THE

FAMILY
FIRST

ENTREPRENEUR

THE
FAMILY
FIRST
ENTREPRENEUR

HOW TO ACHIEVE FINANCIAL FREEDOM
WITHOUT SACRIFICING WHAT MATTERS MOST

Steve Chou

HARPER
BUSINESS

An Imprint of HarperCollins*Publishers*

HarperCollins books may be purchased for educational, business, or sales promotional use. For information, please email the Special Markets Department at SPsales@harpercollins.com.

FIRST EDITION

Designed by Nancy Singer

Library of Congress Cataloging-in-Publication Data has been applied for.

ISBN 978-0-06-326715-2

23 24 25 26 27 LBC 5 4 3 2 1

To my mom and dad, for challenging me to be the best
To my son and daughter, for motivating me to be a better father
To my loving wife, Jen, for being my rock and foundation

Contents

THE
FAMILY
FIRST
ENTREPRENEUR

My Wife Quit Her Job

"I don't want to do this anymore," my wife screamed in frustration as she slumped to the floor, utterly defeated and surrounded by a pile of unfulfilled orders. Jen and I had been running our business for three years now, and by all accounts it was a huge success.

We'd met all of our monetary goals in just a few short years. We'd replaced my wife's income so that she could stay home with the kids, our brand had appeared on national television, and our business was extremely profitable.

But that night, we hit a breaking point.

We had gotten into this mess because we'd lost sight of our vision—or rather, I had. I had confused true success with growth and dollar signs, and our whole family was suffering because of it. When I saw the tears and anguish in my wife's eyes that night, it all became clear. Something had to change.

• • •

My wife cries a lot. I mean, not just when she's upset but when she's happy, too. So when I asked her to marry me several years before that critical moment, we both knew she'd be crying at the altar. To be fair, if I knew I was going to spend the rest of my life with me, I'd be bawling, too. Since we'd already paid an ungodly amount of money for a photographer, we didn't want all our wedding photos to be of my bride carrying around a fist full of crumpled-up tissues. That would've ruined the whole "happiest day of your life" look we were going for. Her crying was inevitable—we just wanted something a little classier than a Kleenex.

Thus, the search for the perfect wedding hanky began.

We wanted one hankie for each person in our wedding party, as well as extras for family members. All we could track down, though, was a cheap set of overpriced pieces of polyester from a local bridal store for $15. We decided to get creative and find our own online, but a web search revealed basically nothing. Keep in mind that this was 2003, so search engines were not what they are now, and the Internet was still a fairly new place to buy and sell things. We didn't give up, though.

After some digging, we came across a factory in China that offered much higher-quality products than what we could find in the U.S. But the minimum order was two hundred hankies. We couldn't find any other option, so we ordered all two hundred, paying fifteen cents apiece (the shipping ended up costing more than the actual product). We only used about a dozen in the wedding, leaving us with 188 extras.

Around the same time, I was selling used electronics on eBay to make extra money. It wasn't a full-fledged business, just a side hustle. Still, it gave me an opportunity to learn about business and entrepreneurship, something I'd always been interested in but never felt confident enough to pursue full-time. What I would do is go on Craigslist, find people trying to get rid of their old computer systems, and buy them; then, I'd disassemble them and sell the parts on eBay. It was my own form of arbitrage; and if it worked for electronics, maybe it could work for other products, too. Looking at the boxes of handkerchiefs, I thought, "I don't know if these are going to sell, but I might as well try."

Within a few days, we sold out. We didn't think much about it at the time, returning to our busy lives and demanding jobs, beginning our life as newlyweds, but this first real foray into business would all come back to haunt us.

BIRTH OF A BUSINESS

A few years later, Jen became pregnant with our first child and wanted to stay home to focus on being a mom. At the time, she earned a six-figure salary, and I was working as an engineer in the ridiculously high-priced Bay Area of California, so we couldn't afford for either of us to just quit. We figured the best solution to making some extra money was to start a business, so we started brainstorming.

The first concept we explored was a meal prep service called Dream Dinners where customers come to your storefront and prepare meals for their families. They assemble dinners with the provided recipes, take the food with them, and cook it at home. It's like take-and-bake pizza but with better ingredients and more elaborate meals. This was a franchise model, and the start-up costs were more than we wanted to spend, so we continued our search.

Next, we considered buying a tutoring center called Kumons, but it was the same as before. Once again, we'd need significant capital to invest in a storefront, pay franchise fees, and run the business. All told, we were looking at a minimum of half a million dollars just to get started. Not to mention all the overhead and operating expenses after that. Other options included a bubble tea shop, as well as a few other brick-and-mortar businesses—all of them dead ends.

My wife and I are naturally risk-averse people, so going into debt to gain greater financial freedom just didn't make sense. We were looking for something with a little more flexibility and security. Granted, starting a business isn't necessarily a "safe" choice, but we wanted to minimize our downside as much as possible. If we failed at our first attempt, we wanted to live to fight another day so we could try again. We wanted a business that was easy to manage and required minimal start-up costs with as few people as possible to run it. We wanted it to *feel* right, as well, as subjective as that may sound. We wanted something that worked for us on a lot of levels and gave us the independence we were seeking without shackling us to another day job. We considered more than a few ideas, but none fit our criteria.

That is, until we remembered the hankies.

In this search for the perfect business, it occurred to me how quickly our leftover wedding handkerchiefs sold and how profitable they were—much faster than the electronics parts I was flipping on the side. When I thought about this some more, it just made sense. We could order another shipment from China, then turn around and sell them at a markup and keep the profits. It felt easy. If the results were the same as before and stayed steady while we increased our order amounts, we'd be able to replace Jen's income in no time. "Let's just see if this handkerchief thing can work," we essentially said to each other.

That's just what we did; and man, did it ever work.

Getting back in touch with our vendor in China, we were surprised to hear they were still in business, so we placed the minimum order to justify another shipment to the States. After that, we got to work, purchasing a domain name and a used computer to get started. I downloaded a free ecommerce platform so that we could start selling directly to customers, and we purchased a digital camera to take photos of our products and put them on the website. We wanted as little risk as possible, investing the absolute minimum amount of money necessary, because we didn't know if it would work. If the whole thing failed, we wanted to be able to recover quickly and try again. All in, we invested $630.

That's how Bumblebee Linens was born.

Once again, we sold out of our initial inventory quickly, but the next time we ordered a lot more, ten times what we had previously ordered, taking advantage of bulk shipping rates by sea instead of plane.

At first, we were selling on both eBay and our own site, but soon we saw that we were making way more money selling directly to our customers. The eBay crowd was trying to bargain hunt and wanted to haggle on every order, or they wanted to find something to complain about. It wasn't worth the hassle.

Selling on our own website, in contrast, allowed us to build a sense of camaraderie with customers and earn their loyalty. Not only were our sales stronger when we stopped selling through third parties, but people really appreciated what we were doing. They would come to us and say, "Hey, you're the only place that sells these anywhere . . ." They were beyond grateful, and we understood why. Not too long before, we were in a similar situation and astounded that nobody else was doing this. Sometimes that's all a business is: a simple solution to a specific need. To this day, we still get emails from people thanking us for what we're doing and sharing their utter shock that there aren't more people selling personalized handkerchiefs online.

Over time, the business grew, and we invested more of ourselves into it. It came to the point where Jen was, in fact, able to quit her job—just as we had planned. After years of running the business and working a day job simultaneously, I was even able to join her. These days, we live a life full of freedom in time and money. We spend most of our time with each other and have plenty of energy and attention to give our kids. Our life, in many respects, is a dream come true.

But before all that, it was hell on earth.

TOO MUCH SUCCESS CAN KILL YOU

In our first year, we made over $100,000 in profit. Our revenue grew in double and triple digits each year after that for the next few years. In the beginning, we had a lot of fun. A few nights a week, we'd stay up late fulfilling orders, sitting in front of the TV chatting while we printed shipping labels and packed boxes. It was a blast. Every now and then, we'd see a huge spike in sales and drop everything in a mad scramble to meet our deadlines. As orders increased, these spikes occurred more frequently, and we started to bicker because of the stress. Jen didn't like the unpredictability of the sales, and I kept wanting more. Eventually, every free second we had was consumed by the business.

Meanwhile, we had an even bigger problem. The bulk of our profits were generated from custom-embroidered products, but my wife, who did all the embroidery, was burned out. Embroidery was a huge value-add, our biggest selling point to customers, so we had to keep doing it. At the time, I was all ambition and didn't know how or when to put on the brakes. What did she mean she didn't "feel like it" anymore? This was nonnegotiable; we *had* to keep going. So I did what any man in my position would do: I learned to embroider.

Okay, maybe not every guy would do that. But I was committed to succeeding, and working harder seemed like the only way to make it happen. Every night, after working ten hours at my day job and then putting our kids to bed, I'd sit down and embroider for a couple of hours. It wasn't how I envisioned spending my evenings as a young father and husband, but it had to be done. I prided myself on my ability to keep pushing us toward success, no matter how hard it got and how miserable we became. My ambition blinded me to what was really happening in my family, marriage, and personal life. I ignored all the warning signs.

On the outside, everything seemed to be going well. We received compliments from friends and family as well as rave reviews from customers. Years of hustle had earned us a gold star in entrepreneurship: the money was coming in, we were starting to receive national media attention, and we just kept growing. Everyone assumed we were killing it, and in a way, we were. But the problem with killing anything is that eventually something has to die.

Our final breaking point came when we were featured on *The Today Show*. *The Today Show*, of all places! It was thrilling to get exposure for our business on such a high-profile media outlet, especially at the time. But I had no idea what it would do to us. In those days, appearing on *The Today Show* for our industry was like being on *Shark Tank*. It was a big deal. Robyn Spizman, who was a regular on the show over the holidays, reached out to us regarding our products. She had found us on Google, liked our products, and asked for samples. We had no idea that we were going to be featured—it was all dumb, weird luck.

When we were finally told that our products were going to be on television, it was November 2013. We weren't given many details and didn't know what to expect. The show would air on December 6, so that gave us a few short weeks to prepare for the increase in traffic and sales. Although our site was ready for the increase in demand, we were not.

I wish I could tell you what it was like to be on this iconic show, bringing national media attention and focus to our business, but I can't. I literally *cannot*. We were only on for something like twelve seconds. That's it. A couple of blinks, a few quick blurbs, and they were breaking for commercial. It was unbelievably short, and as soon as it had begun, it was over.

When the episode aired, our sales increased overnight by sevenfold. The show featured the personalized handkerchief samples that we had sent to the hosts. When I first checked our traffic after the appearance, I saw over two hundred people on our website. That was unprecedented, but then . . . it kept going. Soon, we were getting hundreds of orders every day, each consisting of an average of three handkerchiefs per order, making a total of nine hundred custom embroidered handkerchiefs for us to fulfill every single day.

This went on for a week. It just wouldn't stop. After the first week, the show was broadcast in different time zones and redistributed on syndicates, so we started seeing new spikes every time it aired.

Honestly, as surreal as it sounds, the experience was pretty fun—at least for me it was. It was a ton of work, but I liked the challenge. Most entrepreneurs dream of this kind of break, they wait years for it, and here we were, *living* it! It was exciting to have so many sales in such a short amount of time, forcing us to stretch and grow beyond what we were capable of. As the sales kept coming, though, we were pushed beyond the point of just stretching, and things started to break.

In business, sudden growth you aren't ready for is rarely a good thing. If you scale too quickly, you either have to increase your resources to handle the demand or run yourself ragged to keep up. We did the latter. At the end of each day after the *Today Show* appearance, we had a pile of orders that needed to be fulfilled. Somehow, we pulled it off, but it became more and more tenuous to do so. We kept up with the demands of the business, but everything else fell apart. The personal dynamic in our marriage became so miserable and toxic during this time that we both knew something had to change.

But I wasn't sure that I wanted to give up what we had worked so hard to get.

FACING THE MUSIC

Our breaking point, in fact, had come long before all this. In most cases, you burn out months, if not years, before you end up hitting a wall. It's amazing how long you can limp through a way of life that isn't working because you just don't know any better. So, you keep going. You keep pushing. It takes time for the reality of your situation to catch up, and that's just what happened to us.

Long before the *Today Show,* we would have periods of fast growth with a lot of sales coming in and then scramble to fulfill them. It was uncomfortable for a brief time, but then we'd stabilize and get comfortable again. This always made me a little nervous, because I was afraid we'd had too much of a good thing, and it was sure to go downhill. So, I'd start pushing again. I'd create a small crisis for us to resolve, which felt exciting, but that excitement came with a cost. While my wife was killing herself to fulfill the orders, I was riding high on the momentum, setting even crazier goals.

That year we appeared on the *Today Show,* we were on the cusp of hitting seven figures, and I wanted to put the pedal down while things were hot. A million dollars! I could practically taste it. I wanted it more than anything, certainly more than the health of our marriage or family. Even when I saw the writing on the wall, I didn't know how to stop.

At the expense of leaving money on the table, I couldn't conceive of throwing in the towel. We kept at the business while our relationship atrophied. Jen and I continued to stress each other out, getting less patient with each other, while feeling more trapped in the business we'd built, not knowing how—or if—we could escape.

That's when things started to break. Or rather, *we* did.

In the end, my ambition only served to burn us out. That night when Jen finally broke down, she told me, "This isn't fun anymore. I hate coming in. I'm doing the same damn thing every day, and it's monotonous." She was packing orders nonstop every day and had just had enough. Trying to keep up with my continually increasing goals was running my wife ragged, and I just wouldn't let up. She was the one who had to tell me we had enough and that I could stop striving.

"We make enough money," she told me. "I don't enjoy being here anymore. Why are you putting these crazy goals on both our plates?"

I started to see the light. I had put her through hell, and for what? So that I could tell my buddies I had a million-dollar business? How stupid was that? I had been believing a lie, and it was time to get honest.

A BETTER WAY OF DOING BUSINESS

This is a book about entrepreneurship, but not the kind they tell you about in business school or that you often hear about online. I'm talking about the kind of business millions of people start and run every year. The kind where they dream of changing lives—and do.

You don't have to kill yourself to succeed. You don't have to push and strive for more. You can build a great business, run it well, and enjoy the freedom it provides. It doesn't have to burn you out or exhaust you; in fact, the best businesses are easy to run, because the founder decides on a very strict set of rules and priorities and sticks to them no matter what.

Most of us don't do this, at least not at first, and we have to learn these lessons the hard way (as I did). Appearing on *The Today Show* happened in our sixth year of business, but as I've stated, it hadn't been smooth sailing up to that point. It took a dramatic wake-up call for me to realize how off-purpose we'd gotten. Since sharing our journey publicly on my blog at MyWifeQuitHerJob.com, I've realized I am not alone.

Most business owners don't want to become world famous or ridiculously rich. Certainly, they might not say no to those things, but when you really ask them what their priorities are, it's almost always the same. They want a good life and the freedom to enjoy it. Sure, there are those rare exceptions who have some grandiose vision about changing the world, but if you have kids and a partner, then I'm willing to bet their happiness and the success of your family trumps any personal ambitions you may have for success. If that sounds like you, too, then I have good news for you: You're not alone.

If you struggle to balance these two sides of the equation—your own desire to achieve big things while being present to your family—you are also not alone. So many entrepreneurs find themselves challenged to make sense of these two conflicting desires. I personally know many who deprive themselves of time with their family in hopes of getting some big break later that never comes. What often happens, sadly, is their health, relationships, and lives suffer. If you've paid any attention to the online buzz about entrepreneurship in the past decade or so, this is a story that likely sounds familiar.

Wouldn't it be great if there was another way? There is. It's called family-first entrepreneurship.

THE FAMILY-FIRST ENTREPRENEUR

In this book, I'll share with you an alternative to the hustle-culture nonsense we so often hear about in relation to starting a business. You can, in fact, succeed at business without being a stranger to your kids. You can make good money and have the freedom to enjoy it. You don't have to work eighty hours a week and be a slave to your business just to make it all work.

In the pages that follow, I'll share with you exactly how we did this, what it took to turn the ship around, and introduce you to others who have made similar shifts in their own entrepreneurial journeys. Whether you are just getting started or have been in the game for years, this book will help you create the kind of freedom you suspected was possible but may have had difficulty creating.

Before we get back to my story and how I had to learn all this the hard way, let me share with you the journey we are about to take together—one I see more entrepreneurs undertaking every single day. This book is broken up into two main sections with each chapter offering an insight, lesson, or step I believe is essential to creating a family-first business. Let's zoom out for a second and look at these sections and the lessons contained in each:

Part I will help you get started, showing you that you have everything you need to begin. We'll talk about the common traps entrepreneurs find themselves in, how to reshape your values and priorities around what truly matters to you, and what it takes to get your business off the ground. We'll also talk about skills, niches, and how to make your first $1,000. It's all about starting the right way or restarting if you've gotten off track.

Part II will give you the skills you need to sustain a business. Here, we'll talk about how to grow the right way, what systems and tools you need to save yourself a lot of grunt work, and what to do when you feel like giving up. We'll also talk about time management so that you can enjoy your freedom and surround yourself with those who will challenge you to succeed in all the ways you want.

At the end of Part II, there is a bonus appendix with a short quiz to help decide when to leave your day job and go full-time as an entrepreneur.

This book will walk you through a better way of building a business, one where you don't have to strive unceasingly to succeed—whether you're just starting out or many years in, wondering if all this hustle and grind is really worth it. I believe Family-First Entrepreneurship is the future of business, and it's never been more accessible to those who want it.

My wife quit her job and ended up working harder than she ever had only to hate the business we built together. This is our story of finding a better way. I hope it inspires you to find your own path to success and happiness.

PART I

STARTING

CHAPTER 1

Escaping the Entrepreneur Trap

When I was an engineer, what I liked most about my day job was that it ended. Well, kind of. I'd get home around six, eat a quick dinner, play with the kids, then put them to bed. An hour later, I'd have a call with our team in India to discuss the latest project we were working on, making sure everyone had everything they needed so they could work while I slept. Then I'd go to bed and do it all again the next day, heading off to work while my kids were getting ready for school.

As much as possible, I'd try to make myself available for my kids' activities, but if I left work early, I'd have to make up for it later. Usually, this meant working later and sacrificing sleep. It wasn't an easy life and far from perfect, but it had its own boundaries and rules; and I understood them.

I went to work, did my job, got to spend a little time with my family, and that was that. It was simple and predictable, albeit a bit boring at times. When the job felt tedious or pointless, I'd sometimes catch myself wondering what it would be like to work for myself, envisioning all the freedom I'd have to do whatever I wanted. I wouldn't have to answer to anyone! It sounded like a dream.

This, it turns out, is not how it works when you run your own business.

Some people say that entrepreneurs work eighty hours a week for themselves so they don't have to work forty hours for someone else, and that's true for many business owners. They wear their hustle like a badge of honor, pulling late nights and early mornings for the sake of some big vision or goal. They brag about putting in the hours and burning the midnight oil, but all I hear is a bunch of parents who won't make it to their kids' games and who aren't home in time for dinner.

If you're like me, you've read more than a few books and articles telling you this is just the way it is. You've listened to plenty of podcasts with entrepreneurial success stories telling you that hustle is the cost of admission. But I am here to tell you there is another way.

Most people, I've found, want to do work they love, make good money, and have free time to do what they want. This is not only possible, it's entirely reasonable. Trading your life now for the hope of something better later is stupid, at least for a guy like me who wants to see his kids grow up. I want to be there with my wife each morning and take her out to lunch as often as I can. I want to see my kids come home and hear how their days went at school. I want to go on family trips and stay up late on summer evenings with them, playing outside until sunset. I want my work to make this life possible, not conflict with it. But this is not the way most businesses operate.

Not to mention that the potential "something better" we sacrifice our time and freedom for rarely comes. Sometimes these bets pay off and you win the lottery, but often they don't. What usually happens is you work yourself to the bone, lose what precious time you had to spend with your loved ones, and in the end don't have much to show for it. When it *does* pay off, what you sacrificed is often greater than what you received. You never get another shot at a missed moment, and many early-stage business owners want to squander the only nonrenewable resource they have: their time.

This is what I call the Entrepreneur Trap: the myth that the work you do now will somehow make up for all the experiences you missed along the way. We business owners have this twisted (and unstated) idea that everyone we overlook on our journey to the top will somehow magically understand what we had to do to get there. We silently imagine that, once they see what all this sacrifice helped make possible, they'll tell us with understanding and empathy that it was worth it.

And my friend, let me tell you: It is never worth it.

THE LIES OF HUSTLE

These days, everyone loves to talk about hustle. The social media gurus, podcasts, and business blogs all tell you to constantly do more, push harder, keep growing. They glorify hundred-hour workweeks, calling it "paying your dues" and "doing your time." But for those of us with families, this is crazy. Do you know where you do time? In *jail*. And that's exactly what this kind of imbalanced approach to building a business is: a kind of prison. Hustle entrepreneurship is a trap, tying you down with more work to do, more money to make, and more time to spend away from family. There's *always* something else you can be doing, and it's never quite enough. There's always a cost.

Growth is the holy grail of hustle entrepreneurship, a prize to be fought for at all costs. Whatever your goal was last year, according to this line of thinking, you need to raise it for this year. Flatlining is what hustle fears most. No matter how much you're earning, it's not enough. You can always give and do and make more. The idea here is that if you do these things—if you work hard, sacrifice pieces of yourself along the way, and grow, grow, grow—then the life you seek will be granted to you. The approach with this mindset is that your goal is always growing. It's always located somewhere on the next horizon. And the next, and the next, and so on. Success is never *here*, and so you never stop.

This old formula doesn't work for most business owners, and it certainly didn't work for my wife and me. It doesn't work, because most people don't want to become rock star entrepreneurs. They just want to make good money doing stuff they don't hate and have enough time and energy to enjoy their lives. In our case, hustle entrepreneurship had led Jen and me right back to where we started: to a life we didn't want. And this time it was worse, because we couldn't put in our two weeks' notice.

What a lot of entrepreneurship gurus *don't* tell you is that a life spent chasing after growth often leads to high revenue but little profit. You end up ultimately making less money in the long run, spending even less time with your family, and feeling constantly more stressed and behind the ball. Your business becomes a house of cards that can come crashing down at any minute. This is where we ended up: Instead of running a small, profitable business, our company was now running us. We had to take back control, no matter what it cost us.

THE REAL GOAL OF ENTREPRENEURSHIP

For most of us, it's not about the money. It's about the opportunity to live and work the way we want, to finally call the shots. And for those of us with families, building a business is about more than sharing a helpful skill or product with people who need it; it's about spending more time with the people we love, doing the things that we love. At least, that's what my wife and I were hoping for, and it didn't take long to realize we were getting the opposite.

Jen and I wanted to run our own business so that we could spend more time with our kids, coach their teams, and be home when they got back from school. We wanted to run our lives *our* way and not be controlled by the whims of our employers. Several years into the process, our dreams came crashing to the ground. My wife had less time than before, even though she'd been able to quit her job and stay home. Having to work late into the night when you have young children isn't ideal. We'd created another job for ourselves, with even more constraints than before. It just wasn't working.

To make matters worse, my schedule was beginning to look like my parents' while I was growing up. To some degree, the busy work lives of my first-generation immigrant parents was what inspired me to strive for something different in the first place. I will always be grateful for everything they did. They worked insane hours for most of their lives so that my brother and I could have a better life. I love them for that and try to emulate their example in many ways, but this kind of work life came with sacrifices.

I rarely saw my parents during the week and sometimes not even on the weekends. They were up early and went to bed late. We had a nanny live with us because my parents needed the help. They ingrained in my brother and me a strong work ethic, but I wanted something more than success when it came to a relationship with my kids. I wanted to be with my family, to be present for games and homework and everyday life. Starting a business was supposed to give us this freedom, but it was backfiring, and we felt helpless to fix it.

Most entrepreneurs fall into the exact same trap. They start with a desire to create more freedom for themselves and their families, but somewhere along the way they lose the plot. Every entrepreneur I've ever met has struggled with the question of *enough*. We are always searching for more, wondering if there is a better way to do things. When harnessed and put to good use, this is great. But when we aren't clear and honest with ourselves about what we want, we lose our way. Ego gets the best of us, and we start doubling down on our goals, greedily pursuing more without understanding why. We ask everyone to give to the point of breaking—and they do.

It took me some time to realize what "enough" looked like for us and how I could succeed at business without having to become someone my wife didn't like. Every day, though, I see all kinds of nonsense about how hard it is to run a business and why you shouldn't expect it to be easy. I appreciate the sentiment. Becoming an entrepreneur is not something one should take lightly, but this line of thinking sets us up to believe the myth most entrepreneurs accept without question: that success should cost us everything.

The truth is a little more optimistic. It is, in fact, *possible* to run a successful company and have plenty of time for the things you enjoy. It just comes down to how you build it. Don't buy into the trap of working late hours into the night in hopes of sipping mai tais on the beach later. It won't happen. Hustle entrepreneurship *does* work in the sense that it helps you crush goals and make money, but by the time you are able to enjoy life, you have lost all the moments that would have made it meaningful.

In spite of its challenges, entrepreneurship is still the best way to give yourself the freedom you want. You just have to do it the right way. In my own life and in the lives of others, I've seen how building a family-first business can change everything for you and your loved ones.

Your business should enhance your life, not compete with it. You don't have to hustle or buy into the propaganda you see on social media and hear about in podcasts. You just need to understand how to use a business to create more freedom and stick to your principles. If you are like I was not so long ago with a so-called successful business and a spouse who was becoming increasingly estranged from me, you're not alone. It's not too late. You can still change course and regain control over your life and business. This stuff isn't rocket science, but it takes intentionality to make it happen.

DOING IT DIFFERENTLY

The realization we had succumbed to the trappings of entrepreneurship became clear when my wife and I started making a lot of money but couldn't get out of the business. The first sign of trouble was when we realized we couldn't go on vacation. We couldn't really do *anything*, in fact, outside the increasing time demands from the business. When we left for a short while, we didn't trust the people we had on staff to run the company while we were gone, which was obviously a problem. We'd done all this work to create a life of freedom and stability, and now we weren't able to enjoy any of it.

Another early indicator we were in trouble was when I was at my kids' soccer games and couldn't focus on anything other than the email blasts that needed to go out the next day. During this same season, date nights with my wife became unbearable. I recall one night in particular when we were at a nice restaurant, just the two of us, and all we did was talk about work. Over a very fancy dinner, we were too busy complaining about our factories raising prices and screwing us over that we completely missed our meal. It ended up not really being a date night at all and more like a business meeting. This happened more and more often to the point that it was the norm, not the exception. Sure, we were dressed up and at a fancy restaurant, but it was just more work. Our marriage was in trouble, and we didn't even know how bad it had gotten.

Let me put it this way: When you dream of flying to a factory in China in the middle of nowhere where the food and water is unsafe and the living conditions are horrible—and you start thinking *that's* a couple's getaway—well, then, you really have a problem. That's how bad it got.

During a particularly stressful period in our relationship, when we were just trying to hit our business goals, I was sitting back-to-back with my wife in our office, and we were both feeling incredibly stressed. We were already pretty high-strung because of the huge goals we were trying to reach and the challenges we were facing. To make things worse, one day my wife (for no reason I am aware of) set a stack of important documents behind my chair and I, without knowing what was behind me, immediately rolled back over them, leaving track marks on the paper. She lost it. We started fighting until we could no longer think of another thing to say to each other and just stopped, utterly exhausted.

This was the point when it became clear that our business was causing us both more stress than it may have been worth. Prior to this season of life and marriage, my wife and I had never really fought like that. We used to get along great, but all of that had changed due to the pressures of entrepreneurship and business ownership. Our work had caused all kinds of tension in our relationship, and we were both constantly on edge.

What's interesting about all this is that we already had plenty of money at this point. A few years after we had launched the shop, I had started blogging at MyWifeQuitHerJob.com and began selling online courses, sponsorships, and tools to people who wanted to repeat what we had done with our ecommerce store. Both businesses were profitable income sources in their own right. As each revenue stream grew, though, we made more money every year, and this put more pressure on us. At first, the push was exciting, but it eventually became too much. If we were already set, then why were we obsessed with growth? Who was really in charge of this operation: us or the business? And why did we think more about our company than we did about our own kids—the ones we had supposedly built this business for in the first place?

The moment Jen broke down and told me she couldn't do this anymore, we decided to do things differently. The change didn't happen overnight, and it was far from easy, but finding another way of doing business put us on a very different path from how we had done things before. When my wife called me out, it woke me up and helped me see how hard I was pushing and how much it was tearing our family apart. This is what hustle gets you. We had to rethink how we were doing everything, and that started with going back to the beginning.

TAKING DRASTIC MEASURES

At some point, we made a wrong turn, and we had to get back on task. What's the point of making money and adding value to the world if you aren't able to enjoy it? We began to make some pretty big changes, changes that not only saved our business but also our marriage.

First, we got rid of all our income goals. They weren't helping, and they were arbitrary. I wanted to hit a certain number because it felt good, but often the result didn't change our life one bit. It was just an ego trip for me. The single-minded (read: simpleminded) pursuit of growth was killing our quality of life and burning us both out. It just wasn't worth the cost. We committed to keeping growth on a slow and steady path and not try to scale too quickly.

In place of income goals, we created a new one: for my wife to be removed from the day to day of running the business. Once we had a clear goal that could easily be measured, one that was connected to the quality of life we both wanted, it was "go" time. I am an engineer by trade and a pretty good problem solver, so after setting these new goals I re-evaluated our business methodically, ruthlessly watching our priorities, automation, and margins. I didn't want to end up back there with my wife on the floor, crying.

Then, we started outsourcing. We re-evaluated the role my wife wanted to play in the business and found a way for her to work almost exclusively in her zone of genius. She enjoyed the creative side and didn't need to fulfill orders or do administrative stuff, but that was exactly how she was spending most of her time. We could hire others or create systems for most of that and move the office outside of the house to compartmentalize work and home. I knew how to code and could figure out cheap ways to automate most of our processes so that everything we did online wasn't contingent on our making it happen.

Slowly, we started to reclaim our lives. At first it was scary, because everything we were doing was flying in the face of what we thought was necessary, but we had had enough. It was time for a change, and it was either do this or die. We ditched the script of hustle entrepreneurship and found ourselves building a company we were excited to run instead of one we dreaded showing up for every morning. We knew there was a chance it could fail—but we wanted to create the kind of business we could love.

Today, Jen and I own and operate two seven-figure businesses: Bumblebee Linens LLC and MWQHJ (My Wife Quit Her Job) LLC. My wife spends about half her time working on Bumblebee Linens and the other half volunteering at our kids' schools. Meanwhile, I run the other business. I have time to coach basketball and volleyball for our kids, we haven't missed a family dinner or bedtime in years, and we grab lunch just the two of us at least once a week. It really is possible to enjoy the fruits of entrepreneurship now—not later. You just have to rethink everything you thought you knew.

Maybe you've hit a breaking point, too. Maybe you've set out on an ambitious path to prove something to yourself only to wake up one day with your closest loved ones no longer recognizing you. Maybe you've believed the lies of hustle entrepreneurship, just like I did. If you haven't, and you're either planning to start a business or have already begun, here's what I can promise you: If you're following the standard script for building a business, the one we hear about on social media and from rock star CEOs, your day of reckoning is coming. I hope you're ready for it when it does.

Hustle entrepreneurship promises magic, but really it's snake oil. No one can operate that way for too long and stay happy. Sadly, this is the only model we're seeing and hearing about in the news and on social media. Most entrepreneurs start businesses expecting to find freedom and joy and sadly get the opposite. They make personal tradeoffs for the sake of success and in the process lose sight of what's really important. They forget their priorities, fall out of touch with their loved ones and their health, and burn themselves out.

We have been sold a lie about what it takes to succeed in business, and it's time to find a better way. If we want to live good lives and build businesses we can be proud of, we have to begin by rejecting the insanity of a system that burns us out fast. Instead, we need to embrace a new mindset for business, a whole new way of looking at entrepreneurship. Before you can accomplish your goals, though, you have to learn to think about them differently. Fortunately, there are examples everywhere.

GET OUT BEFORE IT'S TOO LATE

Sally Wilson runs a store called Caterpillar Cross Stitch. As long as I've known her, she's always been focused on growth, and she's doing fantastic, running a successful seven-figure business. Recently, she emailed my wife, writing the following:

> Hey, Jen, how are you doing?
>
> Sorry for the random question. But do you ever get bored or sick of doing the same thing all the time, working with the same products? It's been six years, but I'm so bogged down day-to-day that it's making me not enjoy any part of it. And it all feels the same day in and day out.
>
> Sincerely,
> Sally

"Yes," my wife replied. "We've been there before." And we had. More than once, in fact. Over the years, we've learned how common it is for solo entrepreneurs to paint themselves into a corner and have the thing they once loved now threaten their joy. Sally didn't have any time or extra energy. She was the bottleneck in her business, which is common for someone who also is extremely competent at the skill people are paying for.

In Sally's case, she had employees, but they weren't empowered to make decisions on her behalf. In that sense, she wasn't able to truly remove herself from the business. And that's essential, because you can't effectively run what you are in the middle of. Even though she kept setting goals to somehow get out of the daily operations of her business, her plans never worked out. Caterpillar Cross Stitch was her business, and she dreaded going into the office.

It seems these days you have to choose between working at a pace that feels healthy to you and taking a longer route to where you want to go or hustling like crazy to retire early. As I write this, my wife and I are both forty-seven years old and have paid off most of our house and look forward to paying off the rest and freeing up money to invest. The goal here is to make work optional sooner rather than later. Sally, on the other hand, has a couple of young kids and recently invested in an office building right before she sent that email to my wife. There's already pressure to pay rent on her brand-new office building for the business. It's a lot to manage, and she's not alone in struggling with the constant stresses of the life of an entrepreneur.

We told Sally something many entrepreneurs would consider crazy: We urged her to stop growing. We explained how we optimized what we already had instead of trying to go bigger every year. The results, we explained, were magical. This surprised and delighted her. She had never considered such a thing, and she told us as much. I get it. I, too, am prone to getting caught up in the hype of hustle culture, with influencers touting the importance of rapid growth and scaling. But is all growth healthy? Is it necessary for the betterment of a business? And at what cost? As someone who has seen the toll that chasing unlimited growth can take, I know what I'm giving up and what I'm getting in return. Letting go of the need to constantly be striving for more allows me the luxury of being content with what I have and making the most of it. I still have more than enough time and energy to see my kids' games and enjoy my life. It's worth the tradeoff, trust me.

CHAPTER 2

Family First

Elon Musk is one of the most successful entrepreneurs on the planet, and he works over a hundred hours a week. On the flipside, Sheryl Sandberg says women routinely settle for non-leadership roles because they put their families first. Can you have it both ways? Can a high achiever live a balanced life without making huge sacrifices? The word *priority* literally means "one thing." You cannot prioritize your life and work if you do not know what you value most. As bestselling author and billionaire real estate tycoon Gary Keller writes in *The ONE Thing,* "When you know what matters most, everything makes sense. When you don't know what matters most, anything makes sense." Taking a family-first approach to business is about creating a filter for how you make every single business decision from here on out. And that starts with knowing what's important to you.

To understand our priorities, we have to get real with ourselves. Stephen Covey wrote about this decades ago in the time management classic *First Things First* when he said, "Urgency addiction is a self-destructive behavior that temporarily fills the void created by unmet needs. And instead of meeting these needs, the tools and approaches of time management often feed the addiction. They keep us focused on daily prioritization of the urgent." Most entrepreneurs are addicted to the urgent; it rules our lives. Getting free from this sickness is not easy, but it is necessary. How do you put your family first and make work optional when you have leases signed and bills to pay? What are the necessary tradeoffs to achieve financial freedom? To do this right, you've got to understand that you can really prioritize only one thing at a time. And there is always a cost.

THE FOUR BURNERS

A while ago, my buddy James Clear introduced me to the Four Burners Theory. It's a simple idea you may have heard before, but breaking it down here may hold the answers to most of your work-life balance issues. We neglect our priorities—what's really important to us—by failing to put first things first. The important gets crowded out by the urgent, and as a result, everything we care about suffers. Most people live their entire lives this way, and that makes sense. It's only natural to react to whatever feels like the most immediate need. The Four Burners Theory, however, forces you to think about the priorities in your life and acknowledge when and why you are putting something ahead of something else.

Here's a brief synopsis. Imagine your life is represented by a stove with four burners on it, with each burner symbolizing a major part of your life. The first burner represents family. The second burner represents friendships. The third burner represents health. And the fourth burner represents work. In order to be successful, you have to cut off at least one of your burners. But to be really successful, you have to cut off two. The gist of this is that success is about sacrifice. So, according to this theory, if you want to be an accomplished entrepreneur, you have to neglect one or more of the following: your family, your friendships, or your health. Are you happy with these four aspects of your life? If not, then it may be because you haven't properly prioritized what matters most to you. There's no right or wrong here, only cause and effect. Focusing on one area of life will inevitably pull attention away from another. The trick is to do this intentionally, understanding the consequences.

Since you're reading this book, I'm going to assume you want your family burner turned on high and that you are willing to sacrifice the other three to make that happen. That doesn't mean you can't succeed at all these areas and be a well-rounded person. But it does mean there are certain costs to this game, and you should try to count those ahead of time. For the family-first entrepreneur, the definition of success means having a profitable business but focusing more on family than growth metrics. It means letting go of optimizing your profit margin and getting to see your kid's T-ball game instead. It means knowing when to cut off one burner in favor of the better one.

But this is entirely countercultural and in many ways counterintuitive. This is not what we picture when we imagine "success" in business these days. Take a quick moment and think about the most successful people you have heard about. Do these people live balanced lives? If you look at someone like Elon Musk, clearly the man has turned off two, maybe even three, burners in his life. I love Elon and admire what he's accomplished thus far, but the man is the poster child of work-life imbalance. In a recent interview, he said that quality time with his sons is also spent replying to work emails. He said, essentially, that kids don't need constant interaction, except when they're talking directly, so he can be with them and still be working at the same time. When the surprised interviewer pressed him about checking email with his kids, he replied, "Yeah, absolutely. I mean, not all the time, but a lot of the time. In the absence of that, I would not be able to get my job done."

I've participated in many mastermind groups over the years. If you're not familiar, this is a group of entrepreneurs that meet on a regular basis to provide accountability for progress and to share ideas. Through these interactions with my peers, I discovered that many people whom I consider successful are often not happy with their lives. They've given up so much to succeed in business that they've turned off their other burners—and they often regret it.

Everything comes at a cost. If you want to spend more time with family and friends or focus on your health, then guess what? Your businesses will not be as successful. Because there's only so much time in the day. And your job is to decide what's worth neglecting and what's not. You simply can't do it all. Once you've decided on your priorities, at the end of the day, you will be happy about the things you didn't get done, because they afforded you time and energy to focus on the most important burners.

We all have to deal with these difficult choices on a daily basis, to choose between what we would like to do and what is absolutely necessary. These decisions are never easy, at least not for high achievers who want to do a lot of things and be effective in nearly every area of life possible. Let me ask you: Would you rather live a life that is unbalanced but you kick butt in a certain area? Or would you rather live a life that is balanced but never maximizes your full potential?

It's a hard thing to consider. I ask myself these questions practically every day, because I know I can't have it all, and I know I have to choose. There is no right or wrong answer, per se, unless you simply refuse to ask it in the first place. The wise entrepreneur is willing to ask the hard questions, face the difficult reality, and do what is in line with his values. It all comes down to priorities. What do you value the most? Is it family, friendships, health, or work? You can't have all four.

My top burner is my family. Right now, my kids are like little businesses in themselves, and they require a lot of attention. Over the years, I've spent a good portion of my time coaching their volleyball and basketball teams and helping them with homework. But this is a conscious choice I made long ago. My goal with my kids is to never miss any of their activities if I can help it, because in the long run, this makes a big difference.

When I was a child, my parents worked most of the time. And while I appreciate all of their efforts in raising me and sending me off to a great college, I wish we had spent more time together when I was younger. Kids notice the little things. If you miss a soccer game or an important event, your absence will be ingrained in their memory forever. In fact, the best thing you can do as a parent is simply be present. That doesn't mean stuff doesn't come up and that kids are unable to forgive their parents. We all make mistakes, get busy, and struggle to balance it all. Still, if we as parents can make a conscious and intentional choice to be there for as much of our kids' lives as possible, they will notice and be better for it. Recently, my daughter was in *The Sound of Music* production at her school. I sat in the front row for all of her performances and I know she appreciated my attendance. I love my kids (my wife is all right, too). Now, let me tell you: After the first couple of times of hearing how alive the hills are, I have to admit even Julie Andrews gets a little old. But I wasn't there for the von Trapp kids. I was there for my daughter.

My second most important burner is a tie between health and work. But why health? Prior to my Achilles tendon injury in 2017, health was probably my last or second-to-last priority, but it shot to the top when I realized its profound effects on everything else. If you are healthy, fit, and get lots of sleep, you can increase the intensity of all your other burners and achieve more with everything else!

Your health matters and the more in shape you are, the more you can achieve. I believe the health burner is the key to maximizing all of your other burners. After all, you can't accomplish much when you are sick. When I was out of shape, I used to get tired easily. As a result, I wasn't as productive with work and didn't have the energy to go out with friends. After I switched to a low-carb diet and lost thirty-five pounds, I gained a lot more energy and ditched my frequent food comas. When I tore my Achilles tendon, it was one of the least productive years of my life because I couldn't exercise and I became depressed. Health is the most important burner, because all other burners depend on it! Don't neglect yourself for what you have to do; in the end, it'll negatively affect everything else. Taking even just twenty minutes a day to get some movement in can make a world of difference. I no longer can forsake the health of my body for a few extra minutes of productivity. It is simply not worth it.

MANAGING YOUR BURNERS

My work and health burner are both similar in priority because I can't work efficiently without good health. Back when I first started my business in 2007, this was not the case. It was all about work and money. But now that I make far more than I spend every year, I focus my efforts on projects that give me the most fulfillment. As I've shared, my wife and I purposely don't shoot for exponential growth with our ecommerce store because two things always happen when sales dramatically increase. First, Jen gets stressed out with the increased fulfillment load and supply chain management, especially when it comes to dealing with Amazon. Second, she and I fight a heck of a lot more (which is probably related to the first issue). So it's just not worth the headache.

Instead of exponential growth, we shoot for steady, manageable growth from both a stress and cash-flow standpoint. After all, our Bumblebee Linens store makes seven figures—more than we spend as-is—without even counting the revenue from MyWifeQuitHerJob .com. In terms of my blog, I find it very rewarding to teach others how to sell. I also enjoy public speaking and running my annual event, The Sellers Summit. As a result, running MyWifeQuitHerJob.com actually contributes to my health burner instead of draining it.

Your burners are dynamic and can be adjusted whenever you like. It's helpful to know the order of your priorities when things get hectic. The first burner I turn off when I have too much on my plate is the friends burner. Don't get me wrong: I value my friendships a lot. But when my other burners are going nuts, I turn into a hermit and stop talking to people. When it comes to my best friends, I don't need to talk to them every day, because when we do get together even after a long absence, it's always as if no time has passed. When we started Bumblebee Linens, my wife and I turned off our friends burner in order to become successful right off the bat. We didn't go out, we stopped watching TV and focused 100 percent on our business. I'm pretty sure that we lowered the health burner, as well, because we were both pretty out of shape.

But those burners stayed off for only about a year. You can stagger your burners however you like to keep them running on certain days of the week or months of the year. Just because you've shut off a burner doesn't mean that it has to stay off forever.

For me, the weekdays are my work days from 9:00 to 1:00 p.m. I rarely talk to anyone during those times. Tuesdays and Thursday afternoons are health days where I'll either play Ultimate Frisbee or tennis or go for a run. Weekends and nights are reserved for family and friends. Some people, like my friend and EcommerceFuel.com founder Andrew Youderian, will devote an entire year to going hard on their business and then relax. Your burners are not linear, and you can achieve a lot more with each one by going "all in" for a short period than when you have all burners going on at the same time. The bottom line is that success in life is about tradeoffs. You can't have it all, but you can come close, if you try. The trick is figuring out when enough is enough.

HOW TO (ALMOST) HAVE IT ALL

Is there a secret to keeping all four burners going strong? The short answer is yes, if you are smart. One way to do it is to outsource. In our household, we use food delivery services so that we don't have to worry about making dinner. We also have a housekeeper who cleans the house every other week. This way, we don't have to worry about the hours it takes to straighten up parts of our house and do the deep cleaning we don't have time for, which would take us away from our priorities of family and work. When it comes to business, you can scale your productivity by hiring more employees—or outsourcing to virtual assistants. When it comes to parenting, you can hire a nanny. I'm not saying you have to do any or all of these, just that we all have to carefully choose where and how we invest our time. It is the most limited resource and the only one that can never be renewed. Once a minute, hour, day, or week is lost, it's gone forever. You can never get it back. Think carefully about where and how you spend your time. These days, you can throw money at almost any problem, which will add more fuel to your burners. But this always comes at a cost. Hiring a nanny allows you to do more work at the expense of quality family time. Hiring more employees comes at the expense of human resource headaches. But done correctly, outsourcing is a great way to "cheat" the Four Burners Theory.

The other way to keep your burners strong is by being hyper efficient with your time. By eliminating activities like watching TV, playing games, or just plain goofing off, you can increase the amount of time you have for work, health, friends, or family. The other key to maximizing the burners you've got is by fierce prioritization. When it comes to business, you can increase your throughput by only taking on projects that maximize your gains or make you happier. With Bumblebee Linens, we try to focus on the customers who spend a lot of money and don't complain; and for our store, these customers tend to be event and wedding planners who buy from us in bulk. This is where we want to focus our energy. When it comes to health, I focus on activities that give me the most bang for my buck. I only do exercises that isolate the major muscle groups when I lift weights. I play Ultimate Frisbee, which provides a great cardio workout with a low risk of getting injured—and it's fun!

Overall, the key to maximizing your burners is to work more efficiently and not harder. My greatest struggle has been second-guessing myself as to whether I've maximized my full potential when it comes to work and business. After all, I feel confident that if I put all my chips down, I could create an eight- or even a nine-figure business, but what would I have to give up? Right now, my work is fulfilling, and I make more money than I can spend. With the way my burners are currently set up, I'm happy with two seven-figure businesses. Success in business is easy to measure, but success in parenting is not. Same goes for marriage and any long-term relationships. These areas of life are complicated and require a great deal of energy and stamina. They are also the most rewarding aspects of life, far more so than money or success.

For me, I've chosen my priority, my one thing that everything else falls under. I have decided to focus on family and let the chips fall where they may. And lest you think I'm a crazy person, let me show you how this works.

TAKING THE FAMILY-FIRST APPROACH

By letting go of the hustle and embracing a family-first mindset, you can create a business and lifestyle that gives you and the ones you love the kind of freedom you dream of. It's not difficult so long as you get your priorities straight and stick to them.

Whenever I share our story and the lessons we've learned, the response from a fellow entrepreneur is almost always one of disbelief. I used to think we were weird or special, but since starting my blog over a decade ago and talking about these ideas online and in front of live audiences, I've discovered we aren't quite so unique.

More and more, I see business owners breaking up with hustle entrepreneurship in favor of something more sustainable, something that, pardon the expression, is safe for the whole family. More of us are breaking up with the old ways we've been taught to build a business in exchange for something better. Being a family-first entrepreneur doesn't mean you can't make a great living and still work hard to achieve big things. It just means you are no longer saying, "I'll do that . . . someday." These people make good money, live good lives, and enjoy their freedom. And that's the kind of business most of us want.

If all this sounds exceptional to you, I want to challenge you to question everything you've been told about entrepreneurship. For the rest of this book, I am going to share with you what it means to be a family-first entrepreneur and how to build a business you don't feel like you have to escape from. Not only is this possible, it's easy! But it won't happen by accident. You'll have to focus, be ruthless with your priorities, and commit to this path. In the end, it'll make you happier than most miserable entrepreneurs are—sacrificing everything for the big payoff that never comes. It's time to do things differently, and that begins with you.

But before we get too far, what exactly *is* a family-first business? A family-first business is a for-profit company where the success metric is creating lasting memories and relationships, not just making more money. The family-first entrepreneur optimizes for time over revenue and makes sure that their children grow up to be good citizens and positive contributors to society.

To become this kind of owner, you don't have to get it all right at the beginning. We certainly didn't. You don't need to be particularly smart or even have a lot of money. What we are going to explore in this book is a whole new way of doing business, one where the rules are completely different from what you and I have been told. Every family-first entrepreneur, I've found, tends to follow a certain set of principles that make everything easier:

1. **THE FAMILY-FIRST ENTREPRENEUR TAKES THE LEAST AMOUNT OF RISK POSSIBLE.** Entrepreneurship is often touted as being this grand risk-taking experiment, but most successful business owners I know don't do that. Certainly, there are the renegades out there who "bet it all on black," but the smart ones make small bets that add up over time. We'll cover more of this in the next few chapters, but starting a business doesn't have to be some scary, bold thing you can do. It can be as simple as spending a few hundred bucks on a website and some product just to see if you can sell it. It's a game of chance but there's no reason why you can't play it smart and take calculated risks.

2. **THE FAMILY-FIRST ENTREPRENEUR PRIORITIZES PROFIT OVER REVENUE.** They aren't running a charity, mind you. The goal is still to make money and a lot of it. But many businesses die when the owners or CEOs get greedy about growth without watching the bottom line. This makes sense when you're trying to launch the next Google or Twitter and your valuation is tied more to how many sales you do in a year versus what's left after spending most of the money you've made. But for

the rest of us, what makes a business a success is one thing: profit. When you lose sight of that goal, you run the risk of bankruptcy or working yourself too hard to enjoy the little that's left after paying your bills and taxes.

3. **THE FAMILY-FIRST ENTREPRENEUR VALUES TIME OVER MONEY.** Building a business takes both time and money, and in the beginning, it's often just you doing everything. Soon, though, you realize there is a direct correlation between how much time you spend on certain activities and how much money you make. As the business grows, you may also see that the more money you make, the less time you have. With family-first entrepreneurship, all that changes. Because our freedom is our most important asset, we want to protect it as much as possible. This is why we focus on building systems that work and outsourcing anything you can to the right people. Certainly, there are times when it makes sense to keep a certain task in house, but for the most part, your goal is to get rid of as much busywork as you possibly can so that your business can make good money without your having to work yourself to the bone.

Many entrepreneurs are looking for a silver bullet to make their life dramatically easy overnight. But those who have been in this game for a long time will tell you that such a thing doesn't exist. Not really. Success in business is a mix of good principles, hard work, and some luck. Trying to find the perfect way to do it is crazy. What does help, however, is ruthless prioritization of what matters most to you. This is not as popular as, say, talking about your ideal customer avatar or lifetime value, but it is the most important thing you could do.

No one can tell you what's most important to you. You might not even know until you see your partner on the floor, bawling because of some stupid goal you set. I guarantee you that you'll know then what success is worth and what it's not worth. So many gurus and so-called experts promise big returns while selling you a lifestyle that doesn't work for anyone who wants to experience a vibrant life outside of work. But when we know what to prioritize and what can fall to the wayside, we have a clear path to what we want—along with some helpful guardrails to stay on track. This is how my wife and I eventually created the life we wanted, running two seven-figure businesses on fewer than twenty hours a week while focusing on family.

I am going to share with you exactly what we did, how we did it, and why a whole new generation of entrepreneurs are doing the same. I hope it helps you get the freedom you want without the strife. You don't have to build something you hate in hopes of doing what you love. You *can* have a life and a business you enjoy right now. It'll take a little work, but it's the right kind of work that won't fry you or have you doing stuff you dread doing.

CHAPTER 3

Chase Curiosity, Not Passion

When I first started Bumblebee Linens with my wife, I had zero interest in selling handkerchiefs. After the first few weeks, however, I found myself spending most of my free time learning to design websites so that I could build our site from scratch. When the website was launched, I turned my attention to reading books on marketing and sales. As we started getting more sales, I shifted to researching handkerchiefs, linens, and lace. I even learned to sew! When we started, I didn't think I was passionate about any of this, but here I was: of my own volition learning all kinds of skills that I had never considered before.

The lesson here is simple: Your passion isn't always what you think. You may believe you are interested in a specific field only to one day be surprised by something new that is both interesting and motivating to you. Trust that. After all, engineering, marketing, sales, sewing, and Battenberg lace don't typically go together—but I loved all of it. Ultimately, I became so interested in this business we had started that I launched a blog at MyWifeQuitHerJob.com to document the journey. The website eventually led to an ecommerce course, podcast, and YouTube channel, as well as a live event. And the rest, as they say, is history!

So, what's the point?

Leave room in your entrepreneurial journey for you to surprise yourself. Passion is overrated. Don't be afraid to chase your curiosity and try different things as you explore what could be a tenable business. Did I intentionally create a blog or linens business with the hopes of making a million dollars a year? Hell no! It just happened, but when I saw things coming together, I focused on going all in on these projects. I never set out to do any of this—that's what made it fun. To be honest, making seven figures selling handkerchiefs still sounds kind of ridiculous to me. If you take me back a decade before we started—to being a Stanford graduate and engineer—and told me that I was going to be making millions of dollars a year on the Internet running a small, family-based business, I would have slapped you silly. We humans are not great predictors of our success. This is why we should remain open-minded in our business pursuits. You never know where your curiosity might lead. And curiosity is a far better gauge of success than passion.

PASSION IS OVERRATED

Don't get me wrong. I think passion can be great, but there's just so much more to business than chasing what you *think* will make you happy. Don't start with what you love. That stuff changes, and often. Ask yourself, instead, what you're good at. What skills do you have that you can use to make money? To answer that question, you have to become attuned to hidden opportunities you might not recognize. You have to get curious.

Listen, nobody wants to "burn the boats" of a successful career for a risky endeavor, especially one that may not pan out. So I'm going to be honest with you: Success is not a given. Will you succeed at this new pursuit? Maybe. But you don't have to go "all in" right now—all you have to do is try. The key is consistency. Can you maintain a steady pace for an extended period of time? Can you push through difficult times when you are bored and have no desire to continue? Can you do what most people are unwilling to do and keep going when others would give up? That's what makes the difference for most entrepreneurs.

Those who succeed in business aren't necessarily passionate about their industry or product. In fact, they often aren't particularly exceptional at anything except, maybe, their willingness to not quit. There's no such thing as work you'll never get stressed over, never get bored with, or never complain about. In all likelihood, you're not going to love every minute of working for yourself. Even though my ecommerce store, blog, course, and podcast are successful, there are plenty of times when I hated doing it. Still, I sucked it up and kept on trucking, because the alternative was far less appealing. I was focused on creating freedom for my wife and family and willing to do whatever it took. It wasn't passion that built this thing; it was curiosity and perseverance.

Most entrepreneurs struggle with confidence when getting started, because they believe no one wants to buy what they're selling. Oftentimes, we early-stage business owners are passionate about our product, and this blinds us to the possibility that we may be selling the wrong thing. I often advise new entrepreneurs to focus first on what they're good at instead of what they love. Nine times out of ten, skills trump passion. What you enjoy may come and go, but what you're good at will stick with you for a while. Not to mention, you can always train someone else to learn a skill you've mastered, but you can't easily transfer passion. Just because you like something doesn't mean someone else will. But if you're talented at something, there's almost always a way to make money from that.

People often tell me, "I don't have any skills . . . I can't do *any* of this stuff." It's amazing how often we sell ourselves short, how consistently we undermine our abilities. I bet you're the same. Maybe you're even struggling to figure out what people would pay you for. I have good news for you, though. This is *normal*. It's normal to overlook your greatest gifts, to take for granted your most valuable assets, and wonder what you could offer other people. But that's not how business works.

As Albert Einstein once said so well, "I have no special talents. I am only passionately curious." You don't need to be amazing at something; you just need to stay curious.

When Josh Dorkin started BiggerPockets, he wanted to invest in real estate but kept encountering obstacles that cost him time and money. He started a forum which has grown to become one of the biggest real estate sites in the world. He wasn't a master at the area he was trying to monetize; he just had a desire to learn more about it and to help others avoid common mistakes. This can become a valuable skill in itself. Oftentimes, we don't know how good we are at something or what people will find value in—until we try. So, to begin, ask yourself the question: What do you enjoy? What are some things you like doing? What are you curious about?

You don't have to be the best in the world at something; you just need to identify something that brings you joy. Everyone is curious about something. Recently, I spoke with a younger guy in his twenties, and he said, "I don't have any skills. I don't do *anything*." All he did, according to him, was go to work, come home, and play computer games. As soon as he said that, my interest was piqued.

"What games do you play?" I asked.

"Oh," he replied, "I'm really into Monster Hunter. I spend hours every night playing. I'm kind of obsessed with it."

Excited, I pounced on him: "Okay, great! What do you like about this game? Are you good at it?"

He said he was, and I continued my interrogation, because I saw something he didn't.

"What are some things that you know about this game?" I continued. "Is it a popular game? Do other people play it? How many?"

He said it was kind of popular but a bit more on the obscure side.

"Well," I said, "how many people play the game? And are you better than most people you play against?"

"Yeah . . . probably."

"Okay, well . . . What makes you a good player? Can you write down some tips for beginners, things you've learned from playing this game? Are there tools you use that make you a better player than others? Do you have a special keyboard? What else?"

It was a breakthrough conversation for him, leading to the creation of a brand-new YouTube channel and a whole new platform for him. I wasn't only trying to understand his skills, I was also looking to see where what he enjoyed intersected with the needs of others. I didn't know if any of this was directly monetizable—you never do—but I was trying to dig for gold in hopes of finding some special advantage he could exploit for the benefit of others.

Sometimes the thing that creates value for your business is a specific kind of knowledge. Other times it can be a physical product built by someone else that you sell directly to the audience that has already expressed interest in solving that problem. For example, since this guy now has a YouTube channel with thousands of subscribers watching him play a game, then the smartest way to build a business around that audience might not be some secret tip on how to beat the boss but rather a gaming keyboard that already exists. You don't have to reinvent the wheel; just solve the simplest problem you can.

I teach my students to find products that work for them, something they can recommend to others and make money off of. Often, the fastest way to monetize a platform is by taking something that already exists and either reselling it or creating something similar. Because if people are already buying it, then that means there's demand for it. No need to reinvent the wheel! No need for passion. Focus on skills and demand and you'll find a business worth building.

THE WELL-FED ARTIST

Joel Cherrico is one of the first students who joined my Create a Profitable Online Store course, and after years of consistent work, he has created a solid six-figure business selling something most people think is impossible to make a living off of: art! In fact, I have several pieces of his hand-thrown pottery in my living room right now that I bought off of his website, Cherricopottery.com.

Granted, art is one of the more difficult products to sell online because you typically need to create a following before people will buy your products. Art is subjective in that it doesn't meet an immediately felt need of a customer. So if you are a successful artist, people are buying your work—at least in part—because of *you*. Because they like you and feel like they know you. They trust who you are, what you stand for, and the quality of work you create.

Over the years, Joel has created such an audience and has done very well for himself. But it didn't start out this way. For the first few years, he lived as a starving artist, and it took him years to build a reputation, refine his craft, and learn to run a business. It was tough for a while as he had to learn these early skills and lessons. Nonetheless, once he figured it out, everything changed.

For Joel, the inspiration to sell art online began in college when he failed biology and chemistry, forever destroying his dreams of becoming a doctor. That's when he turned to art, remembering that he'd taken a pottery class in high school and made about a hundred pieces of pottery. He even won an award for some of those pieces. All of this came flooding back into Joel's memory as he debated the age-old question everyone faces sooner or later: "What am I going to do with my life?"

He realized that he was good at pottery but, like any sane person, doubted his ability to make a living at it. Still, he couldn't let go of the skill he had for the craft that kept calling to him. He treated his time at college as an apprenticeship of sorts, working as much as he could to get out of as many classes as possible so that he could spend most of his time on the pottery wheel. By senior year, the reality of needing to make a living hit hard. What about money? What about being able to provide for a family at some point? That's when he took a few business classes to figure out if there was a way to turn his skills into a legitimate source of income.

This took time, of course, but Joel started his pottery business around the same time the Internet started blowing up, and he realized the unlimited potential he had to reach people online—that is, if he took his pottery to more than just craft fairs and art shows. Just a few years ago, everything started to take off for Joel, and he now runs a successful pottery business with several employees that is expanding into other avenues.

Before he became successful, Joel pursued a lot of different routes in hopes of getting his art out in the world. He sold pieces locally for a few years to see how customers reacted to his work in person. He even threw pottery in front of audiences to demonstrate his craft. But the turning point in his business came when he began cultivating a devoted audience through live videos.

When YouTube and Facebook Live were introduced, Joel's skills naturally translated to the Web, and he began performing for people online, captivating them with his skill, craftsmanship, and charisma, all of which led to more people wanting to make a purchase. When you see how something is made and the level of skill required to make it—performed right before your eyes—you are far more likely to respond to a call-to-action that invites you to buy it.

This merging of in-person demonstration and the power of the Internet gave Joel an advantage over many of his peers who stuck with old-school marketing tactics that pre-dated social media and even the Internet. Today, he broadcasts multiple scheduled videos every month, and they're watched by tens of thousands of people. He's had over one million views on a single video before and cross-promotes his work on other people's pages, offering to throw pottery in front of new audiences in exchange for a piece of his art. "Thanks to a simple video," he told me, "there can be a thousand people in my studio at a single time. And that really does translate into a lot more people wanting to buy your art."

Joel didn't have to sell out to build a healthy business as an artist, one that is profitable and successful after years of consistent effort. He also didn't need to starve to create work that he believed in. He only needed to follow his curiosity. This was never a gamble; it was hard work, clear focus, and patience. Joel paid attention to what worked, doubling down on the opportunities that paid, while continuing to keep the long haul in mind.

DO YOU HAVE TO LOVE IT?

I often get asked by friends if running my online store really floats my boat. In fact, most of my friends find it hard to believe that I'm in the linens business in the first place. They don't understand how I can possibly get excited about running such a mundane business selling handkerchiefs and napkins. After all, everyone knows that I love technology—and selling little pieces of fabric is about as far away from high-tech as you can get. What they really want to know is where my passion lies and why I continue to love running my businesses after all these years.

I'm often asked, "Do you and your wife have a burning passion for wedding linens? Do you go on forums for brides and talk all about thread count?" Really, though, most questions people ask are about themselves. They wonder if my business would work for them or if they would just get bored and burn out. It's a good question. And the short answer is no. I am not particularly passionate about what we sell. But I am extremely passionate about our business. And there's a big difference between the two.

Do you *really* need to be passionate about your product to start a business? Do I wake up every morning thrilled to sell linens? Nope. But for me, what we do every day in our business has very little to do with what we sell. And this is true for most entrepreneurs. What makes a business owner successful is not a burning passion for the product—at least, not *just* that. What makes an entrepreneur successful is the ability to run a business well, regardless of what you're selling.

Sure, it's nice to love the industry you're in, but sometimes passion can be a distraction. If you love what you're selling so much, that excitement can blind you from the level-headedness you need to make difficult decisions. Granted, running a business can be filled with a lot of boring stuff, so it helps to be passionate about *something*. But it doesn't have to be what you sell. Don't get me wrong. I believe in our products and the value we provide, but our products don't send tingles up my spine, and I'm okay with that. You should be, too, if you want a business that can support you and your family and doesn't rob you of your joy.

PURPOSE TRUMPS PASSION

My wife used to love embroidery—until she launched a business that required her to embroider for hours every day. Ultimately, it burned her out on something she used to be passionate about. This is the danger of taking a personal interest and trying to make a living off it. You may end up losing your passion when you have to spend all your free time focusing on doing something you used to love for other people in a way that makes them want to pay you for it.

For me, though, the business was always about whether we could make enough money to replace Jen's income. That was the real goal, and every decision we made was oriented around that single objective. We passed up a lot of other opportunities that excited me more than handkerchiefs, but that wasn't the point of what we were doing. The point was: Which business would allow us to have the most freedom to do what we wanted? Everything had to pass through that filter. It didn't matter what we sold so long as we fulfilled our primary goal. *That* was what we were passionate about—the purpose behind the business, not just the business itself.

We settled on wedding linens because it was the easiest way to make a healthy profit. It wasn't that we were linen aficionados, necessarily (though we became pretty handy with a needle and thread, if I do say so myself). It just made the most sense. We knew what our "north star" was and found the type of business that could support our goal. As the store allowed us to accomplish many of our aspirations, I did eventually learn to love it. Which is a significant lesson: If you start with passion, you may never find purpose and burn out in the process. But if you begin with purpose and stick to it, passion will follow.

Today, I get a lot of fulfillment out of delivering a quality product to people who need it for one of the most important days of their life. Passion, in my experience, isn't a good driver of entrepreneurship. What excites you will come and go, as do opportunities. But a clear purpose behind what you're doing will help you weather all kinds of storms. As the famous philosopher Nietzsche once said, "He who has a why . . . can bear almost any how." So, don't listen to someone who tells you that you need passion to go into business. It's not true. I've seen too many entrepreneurs fail following that formula, hyper fixated on passion while neglecting what matters most: a clear goal. Everything follows that.

So what kind of goal should you have when starting a business? You need an endgame. If making lots of money is your primary focus, it'll be easy to get carried away and have your business consume your life. You have to decide from the start what you want, and no one can tell you what your "north star" should be. Otherwise, you'll get distracted with all kinds of shiny objects.

Starting with a clear goal and a path to get there is essential. Since our purpose for starting the business was financial freedom, we figured $100,000 a year would be good enough. We channeled our energy toward starting a business that would allow us to work as little as possible and make only as much as we needed. At the time, I was still working a full-time job, so we weren't trying to replace our entire household income. We just wanted enough money for my wife to stay home. We just needed to make sure the business didn't become another job for her. I was willing to do what it took, even if it meant selling something I didn't care about. That was the goal, and we tirelessly worked toward it.

A funny thing happened, though. As we started growing, I became excited each time a customer entered our store. I would stalk their every move (digitally, of course). I would obsess over their clicks, spending countless hours staring at the tracking software for the business. *Why did they leave the store on* this *page? Why did they abandon the shopping cart just before checking out? Why isn't this product selling?* I was fascinated by the analytics and metrics, everything involved in evaluating our performance. It became an obsession for me. Instead of falling in love with the products, I fell in love with the process. Each day, I was amazed by how many people from all over the country were able to find our little website among the millions of other shops that were just like it.

In addition, I started studying customer behavior and why certain products were more appealing than others. As a by-product of improving our sales, I learned a lot about the wedding and textile industry. Not only did I become an expert in our own products, but I analyzed our competitors and kept up-to-date with various trends in the wedding world. I even developed a persona in our industry and became a "regular" on the wedding and sewing forums. It didn't really matter what we sold. I was interested in our products because it brought us closer to our ultimate objective: *freedom.*

Chasing this goal unlocked all kinds of surprising passions. Of course, it helped that the money started rolling in and I could see the fruits of our labor. The results only further motivated me. I kept learning, finding more ways to optimize the business. Google Analytics became a fixture on my desktop, twenty-four hours a day, seven days a week! That was enough purpose for me to find passion and meaning in the work I was doing. It turns out that you don't need to do what you love in order to love what you do. That's simply a matter of perspective.

DOING WHAT YOU LOVE WON'T MAKE YOU HAPPY

Most people don't understand that whether you start a business around an area of passion or not, most of what you end up doing is not necessarily related to the thing you sell. Granted, there are exceptions to this rule, but very few. In our case, we sell linens, but most of the daily operations have to do with sales and marketing, tracking inventory, and customer service. We could be selling computers, and it would basically be the same list of daily tasks.

Don't start a business because you're trying to monetize your passion. Why? Because you won't be very happy, and it probably won't work. In most businesses, what you end up doing, especially in the start-up phase, is all the stuff required to run just about any business, and usually this isn't what you're passionate about. You may, in fact, begin to associate these mundane activities with your passion itself and therefore grow to resent it. It's just a recipe for unhappiness. If you do find something that you love and turn it into a business—and you're ready to do the work—great! But don't believe the myth that this is something you have to be in love with or that it won't work. That's not true. You can start a business around a lot of different areas of interest and make many of them succeed, if you know what to do. You don't have to be passionate about running a business, necessarily. Just know that this is how you end up spending the majority of your time—doing mundane, boring things every business owner has to do.

It turns out that I ended up loving a lot of this stuff.

A simple goal guided me through a lot of the drudgery of starting a wedding linens business, but then I began to really enjoy the process of building a business. First, I geeked out on all the sales and marketing, which got me excited about customer psychology. I learned that making very subtle tweaks in the pricing of our products could have a profound effect on sales. This appealed to my engineer mind that wanted to figure out how a thing worked, conduct experiments, then measure the results.

Running a business can be fun if you are rooted in your purpose for starting it. You may find there are all kinds of things you didn't know you'd enjoy. For example, did you know that customers are more likely to add additional items to their shopping cart once they are ready to check out? I didn't—until I did! These little psychological mind games woke me up every morning excited to run our online store, and they still do. I never know what new thing I am going to learn.

One of my favorite parts of being a business owner is that every day there's a new problem to solve. If you hate problems, don't start a business, because that's what you're signing up for—an endless supply of problems that you will spend years trying to solve. And each solution in itself will eventually create a new problem. I personally love problems, or rather the opportunity to solve them. Nobody loves tons of chaos, but it can be fun to get up every day wondering what new entrepreneurial challenge is going to present itself. In fact, this may sound a little weird, but running a business is like having your own laboratory with customers as your guinea pigs. The whole experience is an effort in trial-and-error. Do this thing and see how real people respond. Try this, see what happens. Doesn't work? Try something else. You can make a set of tweaks to your website and see how customers react. Then, the next day, or even the next hour, you can do something completely different. As you keep track of the responses, you can make more informed decisions about your business that will help it succeed. Making changes that positively impact sales is extremely satisfying for me, and I've learned a tremendous amount about human behavior from just manipulating a little HTML.

Another activity I learned to love was designing websites. As an engineer who spent many years developing hardware for a living, I had to wait months or years to witness the fruits of my labor. But when it came to creating a website, I was able to get near-instant gratification. I've had a blast managing the website design for our online store. Designing the mobile-optimized version of my website made me giddy for weeks. By changing small graphical elements on our website, for example, I discovered that we could funnel customers to different parts of the site. By simply altering the colors and layout of our store, we could provide a drastically different experience for our visitors and even alter their emotional state. So, again, whenever someone asks me how I can possibly be passionate about wedding linens, I reply that it's not about the product, it's about the business.

If you can find some aspect of your business that really excites you, that is more than enough reason to work for yourself. Remember: Most entrepreneurs end up doing the same thing, regardless of what they sell, so if you have to be passionate about something, make it the business itself, not the thing you sell. Just make sure that whatever you decide to pursue is in line with your ultimate goal. I'll sell just about anything as long as I get to spend more time with my family.

Although you don't need to be passionate about the product you sell, you do need to be confident in the value you provide. Selling is ultimately about providing value, and even if you don't personally love the product, you must be confident that it is bringing value to someone else's life. When it comes to the day-to-day, it's more important that you build a business that uses key skills that excite you than it is that the product aligns with your passions.

Hear me loud and clear: I'm not saying you should sell *anything*. Find something that doesn't violate your moral integrity (don't worry if you're not crazy about it) and that allows you to tap into the skills you already have or are interested in developing. Moreover, find something that intersects your passion with market demand. This, more than any-thing, will allow you to successfully sell the product, even if it doesn't totally fit your personal interests.

LET YOURSELF BE SURPRISED

Arree Chung is an award-winning children's author, illustrator, and international speaker. His books have been named the best books of the year by NPR, *Kirkus Reviews,* and Amazon and are sold in over eleven countries. Arree's entrepreneurship journey began as a series of experiments and it took a few tries for him to get it right. But eventually he discovered a way to capitalize on his art skills to create a profitable business and is now killing it online.

Arree's initial business venture was an ecommerce store called Live in a Story, which he created to bring higher quality wall decals to the market. Most of the wall decals at the time were cheaply manufactured in Asia, and they looked it. As an artist, Arree wanted to create something better and thought that if he could find the right market to sell to, he'd make it. However, he was so focused on his identity as an artist that he missed the opportunity to serve his customers. Spending too much time on the quality of the product and manufacturing and not enough on the marketing and sales, he failed. He also struggled, as many creative entrepreneurs do, to create a high-quality product at a cost-effective rate. It didn't work.

This led Arree to pivot to Storyteller Academy, an online school for people who want to become children's book authors and illustrators. As a published picture-book author and illustrator, he realized that he held a unique ability to provide value and teach others what he had learned. He threw up a casual "Hey, would you be interested in this?" Facebook post and discovered a lot of people were. This led to his first webinar, which four hundred people attended, and then he sold his first online course. From there, he scaled the business into an entire program where you learn to write, illustrate, and even build your own brand and market your work as an author and illustrator. The Storyteller Academy was an idea that led Arree to his biggest business yet.

In 2020, a company reached out to Arree about doing a summer camp for kids, but it was canceled due to COVID. He decided to do something similar on his own, doing it all virtually and offering the first week for free. The setup was similar to his Storyteller Academy and began with an organic social media post to see who might be interested. After generating some initial interest, he quickly put together a landing page email opt-in for the free camp and had three thousand people sign up! It was an experiment and an opportunity to build his email list, but the project took off. When so many parents said they loved Arree's idea and would pay for it, he decided to turn it into a business.

The plan was simple. He would run a paid camp for three weeks, then a free week as a lead magnet (i.e., free giveaway for anyone who came to his site), and the profits would get reinvested into Facebook ads to get new customers. He had an existing customer base to which he could initially market, so he didn't have to invest additional capital into the start-up costs. By his third camp, he had 1,800 customers. Demand increased for his summer camp and he enrolled 4,700 students. It kept going after that and hasn't slowed down since. It took Arree a few tries before he found the right intersection between his skills and the demands of the market, but when he did, it was magic. The same can be true for you, too. Arree tried something he was passionate about, and it didn't work. Then he stumbled into the camp, which was not something he was particularly passionate about, but it was a big hit. One thing led to another and to another. Some of this work he was passionate about. Other parts he was not. The point was that he kept chasing his curiosity, open to the opportunities as they came, and he found lasting success.

CHAPTER 4

The Fortune Side Bet

If you ever see me at a casino, you'll find me at the Pai Gow table. Pai Gow is not the sexiest game in the world, nor is it one that draws a huge crowd. But those who appreciate it enjoy the game for its simplicity, longevity, and potential for a large payout. I've learned to love the game so much that I use the principles of Pai Gow to model my entire strategy for financial freedom.

The simple plan I'm about to describe has allowed me to create multiple successful side hustles and achieve financial freedom. Both my wife and I no longer rely on a day job for income, and barring any major catastrophes, we are financially secure. Before you can understand the lessons I've learned from Pai Gow, however, you must learn how the game works. Here is a quick description of the rules:

1. You and the dealer are dealt seven cards. With these seven cards, you create two poker hands—a two-card hand and a five-card hand.
2. Both your hands go up directly against the dealer's two hands.
3. If you win both poker hands, you win the bet.
4. If you lose both, you lose.

5. If you win one and lose one, you tie and no money changes hands.

That's it. But here's the thing: More than half the time you end up tying with the dealer and no money changes hands. In fact, I've literally sat at a Pai Gow poker table for hours and not won or lost a single dime! Given the slow nature of the game, how can you possibly win money if you're "pushing" (i.e., tying) with the dealer more than half the time? How the heck can you hit the jackpot playing such a boring game? The secret lies with the fortune side bet.

Whenever you play a hand of Pai Gow, you are offered the chance to put some additional money in a side pot that pays out like a slot machine depending on what hands you're dealt in the regular game. For example, if you happen to get a straight flush, you win a large sum of money. Even hands as low as three-of-a-kind pay out a decent multiple of your bet. And if that weren't enough, you can still win if a different player at the table gets a good hand, as well. Even though you "push" with the dealer more than half the time and you rarely make any money on the regular game, you always have the chance to win a huge payout. The regular game is super slow and boring, but the advantage is you can play for a long time without losing money.

Pai Gow is an excellent analogy for a day job. A regular day job is great for paying the bills and making ends meet, but you will *never* make life-changing money by working for someone else. Even if you were to go above and beyond and make your company a lot of money, your potential upside is capped by your steady salary. That is almost always true in a standard nine-to-five job. On the other hand, the fortune side bet is where it's at. By placing a small side bet on the table, you have the potential to make a thousand times the money you would earn otherwise in a game of Pai Gow. The catch is you have to risk a little money to play.

In the "real world" (i.e., life outside the casino), your fortune side bet is starting your own business. You might not win on your first try, but the longer you play, the more likely you are to succeed. If you languish on the sidelines, however, and stick with the regular game (your day job), you'll never get anywhere. One of the reasons I love Pai Gow is I can go to the casino and play all night without losing my money. My ability to last a long time gives me enough runway for a chance to hit the jackpot! That's why I kept my job for so long while building two online businesses. It minimized my risk and maximized my upside. When it comes to creating the life you want for yourself and your family, you don't have to "bet the farm" or "take the leap." You can simply place a fortune side bet.

A GAME OF (LOW) RISK

One of the questions I often get asked is whether or not you should quit your job cold turkey to pursue building a business full-time. My response is almost always, "Heck no!" Ideally, you should keep your day job until you've had a chance to fully validate your business idea before taking the plunge into full-time entrepreneurship. After all, running a business is challenging enough as it is; you definitely don't want financial stress to cloud your judgment or make difficult decisions any harder than they need to be. Even though you might hate your job and can't stand your boss, think of these circumstances as a way to stay in the game.

If you keep your job, you can use your salary to buy yourself extra time until you can grow your business into something healthy and sustainable. You don't have to trade one set of stressors for another, which, sadly, is exactly what most entrepreneurs do. They take all their unhappiness and lack of fulfillment in their day job and immediately transfer it to their new gig. You don't have to do that. Instead, you can experiment with a number of different ventures on the side, capitalizing the whole thing with your own money, and see what works. You can, in a way, become your own venture capitalist without having to deal with the song-and-dance of keeping investors happy.

When it comes to starting your own business, the safest strategy is to keep your day job, at least for now. Stick with something steady until your side project gets off its feet, then you can go "all in" if it makes sense. Your family will thank you for this, I promise. It might mean a little extra work for you, but it'll mean a lot more security and a lot less financial stress in the long run. Overall, there are no guarantees with any business, but one thing is for sure: The more time you have to validate a business idea, the more likely you are to eventually succeed. The best and safest entrepreneurial strategies involve creating a safety net and having the freedom to take small but calculated risks.

The biggest misconception about entrepreneurs is that they are all inveterate gamblers. At this point, I've interviewed well over four hundred successful small business owners on my podcast, and I can tell you that not one of them has ever struck me as a big-time risk taker. Quite the opposite, in fact. I don't know if the media is to blame or just some modern misunderstanding about what it takes to succeed, but there seems to be a myth in our culture that successful entrepreneurs enjoy taking wild chances, that they are "high rollers" who go big or go home. In my experience, nothing could be further from the truth. Almost every entrepreneur I've interviewed or met in the past ten years has taken a methodical and conservative approach to starting their businesses. And as a result, most of them have succeeded.

To put it succinctly, what successful entrepreneurs do, more often than not, is take small, calculated risks. They don't bet the farm, which gives them room for little mistakes. Then they iterate. When my wife and I started our business, we both worked full-time jobs while building an ecommerce store on the side. We made small bets as we went, making little tweaks with each step, and learning along the way. Our success is not a result of any brilliance on our part, just a willingness to keep experimenting and not going "all in" too soon.

How did things end up? It took a while, but our store is now making over a million dollars a year. My wife and I no longer work regular jobs, and we spend most of our time with family—not on the beach, sipping margaritas, but with our kids, creating meaningful experiences. What ended up happening was something less than the ideal but something better than what we would have called realistic. In other words, taking our time, making small but calculated risks paid off big time.

DOING BUSINESS RIGHT

I don't want to paint the wrong picture. My wife and I are not rich, at least not in my mind, and we still have to work to make a living. But the nature of our work is much more flexible and rewarding now, and we have gotten what we wanted, which is a life where we are more in control and have the time and freedom to do what we want while making an above-average income.

What's cool about running your own business is that success begets more success. Once we won at one thing, it became easier to stack more successful projects on top of that. When one business became the "steady gig," we were able to place other side bets. Once our online store started bringing in a good income, I set aside some of the cash to start MyWifeQuitHerJob.com on the side. Within three years, my blog started to take off, and I invested some of that income to start an ecommerce training course. When the course started making money, I took some of that money off the table to start a podcast. From there, my podcast led to a conference; and today, I'm in the process of starting two more businesses! Success begets success. Sticking with a steady thing gives you freedom and margin to try new things. There's always another side bet you can place if you stay in the "main game," however boring it might seem at the time.

Almost everything you've heard about entrepreneurship is wrong. If someone told you that you had to "go all in" or that you've gotta "risk big" to get the big rewards, don't believe them. I am sure those people exist, but other than the random life coach on Instagram, I've never met them. Their lifestyles don't reflect what seems realistic or attractive to me and the people I know and respect. Even if that way of building a business is possible, why would you want to risk it all if you didn't have to? That just seems stupid. The odds are you will never make life-changing money unless you play the fortune side bet. It may take a little more time and energy, requiring a little more patience on your part, but it'll be worth it. I've seen this happen over and over again over the years, and the end result is a sustainable, long-term business that provides a tremendous amount of freedom and security for you and your family.

In real life, a fortune side bet is your business, your new venture, or whatever side project you are excited about. Starting a side hustle doesn't have to be risky. Entrepreneurship doesn't have to be "all or nothing." It really can be a slow-and-steady process of taking risks, yes, but not ones that will financially devastate you if something goes sideways. If you decide to take the plunge into business ownership, I applaud you. It's not for everyone, but the rewards can far outweigh the risks, if you do it right. Just make sure you have a backup plan. Stay at your day job until your side hustle can support you. Then, build upon your existing successes until you have a portfolio of income streams.

Take my former student Ming Wang, for example. Ming noticed a need in the women's clothing market when she was pregnant and working as an executive, leading a team of seventy people. She needed to look professional but still be comfortable. Growing a baby and staying in business is hard work, and clothes shouldn't get in the way of that. Ming put her engineering and product management experience to use and began designing and selling maternity pants on Amazon.

Now, three years later, she owns Alina Mae Maternity, which generates millions of dollars per year. She has since quit her nine-to-five job and works on her business eight hours a day, but on her own time—freeing up the afternoons and evenings to spend with her kids. Her fortune side bet turned into a full-time business that has continued to expand. She's no stranger to hard work, but she's also no stranger to her family—and that makes all the difference. Today, Ming is working on starting other businesses and a non-profit, all made possible by selling some pants on Amazon.

DON'T QUIT YOUR JOB JUST YET

See if this sounds familiar. You start a new job, work hard to establish yourself and build your reputation, but then you get bored. At first the nature of the work is challenging. You are constantly learning and trying to keep up with your colleagues. You find yourself staying late at the office just to get by, and part of you loves it. It's energizing and fun and full of life.

As time passes, though, you get better at your job and find ways to do your work faster and more efficiently. You become proficient, an expert at what you do, and with this proficiency and expertise, you relax a little. As more time passes, you feel comfortable and at ease with your job. You are able to finish your work in an eight-hour day with more free time to spend at home. Things become cushy. You get a little bored and wonder, "Is it time to leave?" Maybe you already know the answer and it's just a question of *when*.

But I would caution you to not do that. Not yet. This is the perfect opportunity to start something on the side. Don't go all in at this point. Place that fortune side bet while you still have a sure thing going. Just because you know that you won't be working for someone else forever doesn't mean it's time to jump ship. Starting a business is a process and knowing what to do when is half the battle.

Recently, I was chatting with a close friend about complacency at the workplace. He recently quit his job to join a company that builds completely different products than those of his last firm. Though the nature of his work is similar, the culture and pace of this new company is a brand-new experience. Inevitably, he will have to work longer hours.

So I asked him why he changed jobs. After all, he has a wife and child at home, both of whom he loves spending time with. His former job was a nine-to-five type that gave him plenty of time at night to hang out with his family. He never had to work weekends, and the job itself was pretty low-stress. Why did he give up all that for a new job where he'll have to work more hours and re-establish himself in a new environment? Why sacrifice additional family time for a gig that is even more demanding?

My friend told me that he has a policy when it comes to work. He never stays at any company longer than three or four years, and he'll leave even earlier if he starts to feel complacent. He describes his job-hopping behavior as an itch that develops when he stays anywhere too long, and it can only be scratched by switching companies. In short, he always leaves his company if one of the following is true: (a) he's not learning anymore, (b) company politics are getting in the way of work, (c) he's getting bored, or (d) he doesn't feel like he needs to challenge himself anymore. Those seem like good reasons. Why stay at a job if you feel complacent? That is certainly a valid perspective and approach, and while I agree with all his reasons for switching, I can't help but feel as though he's missing out on a completely different opportunity.

If your current job pays you enough to support your family and it provides you with lots of free time, why not use that free time toward your financial independence? Why take on another job that will make you work longer hours for someone else? At the end of the day, those additional hours of work at the new job are still going toward benefiting someone else. Those extra hours are not going to put more money in your bank account except for maybe a small raise. In other words, cushy doesn't have to mean boring; it can, in fact, mean opportunity.

If you ever want to break out of the rat race and become your own boss, there's no better time than when you have a cushy job. I'm not saying that you should slack off in any way, just that this is a tremendous chance to get ahead without having to burn the boats. You should still perform at your peak while on the job. But finish your work as quickly and as efficiently as possible so that you can go home and work on your independence.

For what it's worth, I continued working in my job for four years after I was already making decent money with our businesses. That's because I enjoyed what I was doing. I was doing interesting work with interesting people, and I wanted to stick with it for as long as possible. It wasn't about the money. As business kept increasing for our online store and my blog, however, I decided to drop down from five to four days a week at my job. Then, after a while, I dropped to three, which allowed me to keep my health benefits. Then I decreased my weekly workload to two days, then one. And finally, I quit. I was one of the top three engineers that designed the entire product that was making most of the money for the company, so there was some privilege there. But why was I the best? Because I loved what I was doing. This is the secret: Love what you do, keep doing what you love, and you'll always have options.

The reason I quit my job was that, ironically, my boss left to start another company. The new guy who replaced him came in and pulled me into the office to say, "I noticed you're only here one day out of the week. What exactly do you do?"

I said, "I'll be honest with you. I don't do anything here." At this point, I didn't care anymore and didn't need the money. I wasn't going to lie to the guy. "I go to meetings and if anything breaks, I'm kind of like your insurance policy," I told him. He was not impressed by that, and I don't blame him. After that conversation, I left my day job.

Honestly, I would have stayed if it made sense. Working one day a week there was ideal for me—I often miss my team and the experience of being in that office. I would go back if I could and sometimes think about it. But there comes a point when it becomes obvious that it's time to move on, and that was it for me.

Quitting your job doesn't have to be some big dramatic moment and oftentimes should not be. It can simply be a gradual choice that just makes sense. If you do it like this, slowly and on the side, when the time comes to quit, you'll be ready, making that inevitable transition much easier.

WORK IS NOT THE ENEMY

Don't make this about quitting your job; that's not what we're talking about here. Lots of wannabe entrepreneurs spend their time trashing "jobs" and work and brag about how little they work. That's not what I'm saying. Work is not the enemy. Doing stuff you hate, spending a lot of your time away from the people and things you love, is what we are fighting against.

The goal of this book is to help you figure out what you enjoy in life, and find a way to spend as much time doing it as possible. That's what family-first entrepreneurship is all about. If you enjoy your job, stick with it. If you don't like it, find one you can enjoy. Then, slowly grow a business on the side that allows you to have more freedom in the long run. Don't neglect this second step, because having a profitable business gives you the option to do what you want and will offer you the most leverage in the long term. I prefer working for myself over working for someone else (most days), but it's still work—and there's nothing wrong with that.

"But wait, Steve . . ." you might be wondering. "Why become an entrepreneur at all if working a day job is so great?" It took me many years to realize that my steady day job was not that steady. When I was an engineering director, I was making a healthy six-figure salary, and this was enough money to pay my mortgage and all my bills. The temptation of a steady paycheck pretty much eliminated any desire to start my own business for the longest time. After all, why should I risk my own money and time when I can get a "guaranteed paycheck" from month to month? You may have thought the same thing. The problem with this thinking is that your paycheck is never guaranteed and it can disappear almost in an instant.

Having worked in Silicon Valley for twenty years, I've lived through two major recessions, the dot-com bust of 2002 and the financial crisis of 2007–2008. During those periods, I saw many of my colleagues get laid off from their very cushy positions in major Fortune 500 companies. And that taught me a crucial lesson: No paycheck is safe. There are no guarantees. Running a business and working a day job each carry their own risks and respective rewards.

Having worked a day job for over twenty years and run multiple businesses for over a decade, I can definitely say that running your own business carries far less financial risk in the long run. I know that sounds crazy, but it's true. Whereas you can lose 100 percent of your income overnight with a job, you will rarely experience the same outcome with your own business even in your worst year. The most likely scenario in the event that you fail is that your business will decline gradually, giving you ample time to plan ahead and find other sources of employment.

Quitting your day job is often viewed as the end goal for entrepreneurs, but the truth is that a better goal is waking up every day to a life you can appreciate and enjoy. If that includes a day job, great. Again, the objective is freedom and happiness, not bragging to your friends about quitting a dead-end job. If you're in a job you hate, that's your fault, not the job's. Seek fulfillment in your work instead of chasing after the "next best thing." Each new job will always bring more work than you expect, and quitting cold turkey to start a business places undue stress on the fledgling business that often requires years to succeed. Look for ways to maximize your own happiness wherever you can, and you'll never feel like a failure—no matter what you do for work. Just know that working a day job will rarely result in life-changing money, but it can provide the stability you need to get started as an entrepreneur.

This work I do now fulfills me in ways I never expected, but I'm glad I took my time getting here, making small bets as I went instead of going all in at once. Recently, a student of one of my online courses contacted me, thanking me for my course on helping her build an online store. She told me that four years ago, she had been sitting on a park bench, having lunch with a colleague, dreading her life and every Monday having to go back to work. She's since created an online store that makes mid to high six figures per year. She followed the steps in this book, quit her job, and found something she could love doing. It completely changed her life, not because she left something she hated—but because she found something she loved.

EXPLORING POTENTIAL SIDE BETS

When I was a kid, I always tried new things just for the heck of it. I never thought about it too hard, just went with the flow and followed my interests wherever they took me. One summer in particular, I spent my break from school reading the encyclopedia all day, every day. Why? I was just curious about all the cool facts hidden in these massive tomes. Another example was when I spent hundreds of hours creating the ultimate Legend of Zelda strategy guide on a typewriter. I also played Street Fighter II for eight hours a day so that I could beat my friends at it.

In other news, if it's not already obvious . . . I was a nerd. I mean, I spent hours learning origami just to entertain friends and family. I may have had slightly warped ideas about what it meant to be cool, but the point is that no one ever told me to do these things. I just did them out of pure enjoyment; in fact, chasing my curiosity seemed natural to me. My parents didn't force me to do these things; my teachers didn't recommend them. I just did them. And the best part? If I didn't feel like doing something anymore, I stopped. I never wondered whether it was a good use of my time. I never pontificated about whether or not I could make money from it. I just did what I wanted and stopped when I lost interest.

So let me ask you: Do you remember what that felt like? To be a kid? To be so curious about life that you were willing to chase all kinds of crazy interests simply to see what lay on the other side of developing a new skill? Remember when most of your time was spent playing? Do you remember pursuing an activity for the very love of it instead of wondering how you might monetize it? Can you think of the last time you went with the flow and chased something that interested you merely because you found it fascinating? What happened to that kid? Where is that person today?

Joe Jitsukawa of JustKiddingFilms and his buddy Bart decided to put up silly videos of themselves on YouTube—just for kicks. They had no intention of making money; they just loved being goofy on camera and wanted to share it with other people. Fast-forward to today and they now make millions of dollars putting out videos they would have produced regardless. It's amazing what you can do when earning an income isn't the most important goal. And I would say for family-first entrepreneurs, money should never be the primary goal. We aren't chasing money so much as opportunity. But this isn't the same as pursuing your passion—not necessarily.

How do you find a successful business idea? Start by getting back to what you were doing as a kid: having fun and trying out lots of ideas that interest you. Don't put all your eggs in one basket or bet the farm on something you think will work—it might not. Make a lot of stuff, play in a lot of "sandboxes," and see what happens. Don't be too attached to the money, especially early on in your journey. Find something that's fun and see where it takes you, like Pete Sveen did. Pete was passionate about doing woodworking projects around his house, so he documented his work on YouTube and now makes a six-figure income online. Large companies like Ryobi, QuickCrete, and Gorilla Glue routinely sponsor his episodes for thousands of dollars apiece. These are just a few stories from countless examples I've encountered over the years. Building your own business doesn't have to be some master plan; it can be fun and experimental.

Building a successful business is one part intentionality and one part curiosity. It's a blend of smart, focused choices and happy accidents. As Jim Collins shares in *Great by Choice,* all leaders get lucky, but the great ones get a "return on their luck." That is, they follow their interests, experimenting as they go, and chase the stuff that works. When they see something take off, they maximize that luck and make the most of it. It's not that they're necessarily any smarter, more talented, or luckier than their competitors; it's just that they know what to look for and aren't afraid to chase it when they see it. Again, it's a lot like playing the fortune side bet in Pai Gow and knowing when to play it safe and when to maximize your potential winnings.

Most of the entrepreneurs I've met over the years became successful simply because they put themselves out there with zero intention of making money but somehow "fell into" a great opportunity and did something with it. Because they were passionate about what they were doing, they didn't consider it work, and money was never the primary motivation. In a sense, they were playing, just like children. My Stanford buddy Eric Cheng was passionate about underwater photography, so he decided to create a website called Wetpixel.com as an outlet for his hobby. That was his initial goal: to just have a place to have fun and share. Within several years of starting the website, though, he established the largest underwater photography community on the Internet. Money started pouring in, and he didn't know what to do with it. He became an entrepreneur by accident.

JUST TRY

Your childlike wonder doesn't have to end just because you grew up. What is it, after all, about adulthood that seems to ruin almost everything that used to be fun and interesting? When exactly did we decide to stop taking action on the very things we loved because we're simply burdened with more responsibility? Did we forget what it meant to enjoy the little pleasures, just because we've got mouths to feed now and mortgages to pay? Many of us, in fact, did just that. But it doesn't have to be this way. Life doesn't have to be an endless grind filled with one form of drudgery after another. Work can be fun. Families can be more than an obligation. Business doesn't have to be so boring—so long as we can learn to rekindle the wonder and imagination of a child. And sometimes this takes a little work, but it's worth it.

The other day, I received an email from a reader asking what he should do with his life:

Steve,

I work a full-time job that I hate. I desperately want to start my own business but I have no idea where to begin. Can you be my mentor and help me get started? How do I find my passion? What should I do next?

Thanks,

Tom

As an Asian male growing up in a tiger household, I understand first-hand why people like Tom hate their jobs. Most people ignore what they are interested in, because they don't believe it's viable. In their minds, their passion or interest is simply not an option when it comes to starting a business. And because of this, most people are simply too afraid to try.

Imagine saying to yourself, "Man, I love Battenberg lace wedding handkerchiefs, but I had better become a lawyer, because that is what is going to pay the bills." Then three years and a hundred and twenty thousand dollars in debt later, you hate working hundred-hour weeks, being a slave to your law firm's partners. By the way, I apologize to all lawyers out there. It's just that out of all my Asian friends, almost all of them hate being a lawyer. So they're easy to pick on. But the point is the same: Most of us choose a vocation because it's the safe option, the one that is less risky than doing what we really want. You know what I'm talking about, the thing that still burns inside you, that lingering curiosity. The deep passion that just won't go away.

But let me ask you: Whose fault is it that you ended up here? Who can you actually blame? If you hate your job, the *real* problem is that you are artificially limiting yourself to some preconceived notion about success that your parents or friends or maybe even society at large has instilled in you. And you agreed with them! Nobody made you pick this path. Even if your parents gave you the money and told you "Become a doctor or we're disowning you," you had a choice. Maybe it was a hard choice, one you didn't want to make. But you chose, nonetheless. And here you are, living with the outcome of the decision. Are you happy? Is it still working for you? If not, it's time to change—and thank God, there's still time to change!

I get a few dozen emails like the one from Tom every week. I know I'm Chinese and all, but for some reason everyone thinks I'm Confucius. If selling handkerchiefs online qualifies me to be a philosopher, then so be it. Chou-fucius says . . . you already know what to do next; you just haven't realized it. All you need to do is become a child again.

Remember when you were a kid and you didn't care what people thought or if some passion of yours ever amounted to a paycheck? That child still exists. That person is still a part of you, and if you want to re-align your life with what really matters, you're going to have to embrace this part—maybe for the first time in a long time. If you don't mind, I am going to get a little nosy now, but it's for a good cause. Don't worry, I'm not going to tell you to stop having fun. Quite the opposite, in fact. If I may, I'd like to ask you a few questions.

First, how are you spending your leisure time? What do you enjoy doing that doesn't feel like work? Have you ever tried to do anything with that? "Steve," you might say, "I like playing video games all day." Or: "Steve, I like reading romance novels whenever I have free time." Or: "Steve, I like to eat out at restaurants . . ." And, at this point, you may be wondering, "And how the hell can I turn this into a business?" I'm glad you asked. My response is always the same: *Well, have you ever tried?* Your problem isn't about finding your side bet. The real problem lies with your priorities, your productivity, and your confidence that you can ac-tually make money doing what you enjoy. So let's address these one by one:

- Have you ever tried to do anything about your interests?
- Have you ever tried to document your knowledge on a blog?
- Have you ever tried to express your opinion through a podcast or video?
- Have you ever tried to make your mind accessible to the outside world?

If the answer is no to all of these questions, then sorry. You have never tried to pursue your passion. Period. You can't complain that your interests are worthless until you've given it an honest try. You've got to become a kid again and become more comfortable with failure, with trying. Kids don't worry too much about failing. They try stuff that looks fun and keep doing what works, what feels exciting and interesting to them. Sometimes they're good at it; sometimes they're not. But they never stop trying. That's how they find where the fun lies. And who said you had to be the world's best at something to keep doing it? Most entrepreneurs I know aren't offering the world's best product or service; if that's what qualified you to start a business, then there would be no competition.

A successful entrepreneur finds their competitive edge, whatever it might be, and sticks with it. The point isn't to be the best at everything; it's to find something you enjoy, and get good at that. Find a unique advantage and exploit it. But before you do that, you're going to have to try many things. You don't need to be an expert, just expert enough. For example, if you like playing video games all day, I'm willing to bet you're "expert enough" to influence other gamers. If you like eating out, there's probably a group of people out there who want to know what you think about a particular restaurant or cuisine. Start sharing your knowledge, without any expectations, and I promise you: Good things will come.

The medium doesn't matter. What matters more is that you keep at it. Just put yourself out there, and document your thoughts as you go. Someone will find your work. Philip Wang, for example, co-founder of Wong Fu Productions, decided to make short films for fun with his friends. This was before YouTube and the digital media revolution we are now experiencing. "This was before smartphones," he told me in an interview. "We were on RAZR phones, okay? And I was like, it would be so cool if someday you could just put a quarter into your desktop or something or . . . scan your credit card, just to watch one of our videos. Imagine if the technology existed, we would be millionaires. And now that literally exists . . ." Some of the films Philip and his friends produced eventually became hits, which led to a full-fledged business with all kinds of opportunities for his partners and him to succeed, including physical merchandise, brand partnerships, and beyond.

Today, Philip is a full-time creator, reaping the rewards of the years of work he and his team put in. But if you ask him, he doesn't consider himself a good YouTuber. For Wong Fu, it's not about chasing the latest fad or trend. Their success is due to the buy-in of their audience and the willingness of the founders to stick to what they're curious about.

"We just always made what we wanted to make," he said, "and that's a testament to how great our fans have been . . . People were following our purpose. They weren't following us for just some trendy thing." What started out as something fun and interesting eventually became a business, because they kept chasing their curiosity, something they continue to do today.

That's how this works.

CHAPTER 5

The Art of Niching Down

Figuring out what to sell is tougher than it sounds. Just because you're good at something or passionate about it doesn't mean anyone wants it. And even if they want it, that doesn't mean they're willing to pay you for it. So this is a process of trial-and-error: finding out what people want, what they're willing to pay for it, and how you can deliver it to them in a profitable way. That's business, and the best way to start is not with what you want to sell but with what people want to buy.

Whether it's something you create, a special piece of knowledge you have to share with the world, or a service you want to provide, picking the right product can make or break a business. The mistake many early entrepreneurs make is they focus too much on the product instead of on the audience. Placing the right bet isn't just about what you sell, it's about who you sell it to. You want to choose wisely when it comes to picking a product, and it usually helps to start small. That way, you can pivot as you go, making adjustments along the way without investing too much effort or money up front.

You never want to sell something that is available to everyone. If you see a product in Target or Walmart, chances are that it's probably not going to be a good fit for your business. That thing has already gone mainstream, and it's going to be hard to compete with. Don't take your entrepreneurial cues from Shark Tank. Instead, focus on offerings that are being overlooked by "the big guys." In other words: *niche down*.

When I meet folks who are starting a business, I often advise them to get as specific and small as possible. It's a little cliché in the entrepreneurial community, but clichés exist for a reason: niching down is the smart way to start. You can always broaden as you go, but you don't want to be what marketing guru Seth Godin calls "a wandering generality." You want to offer a specific solution to a deeply felt need. When my wife and I found high-quality handkerchiefs halfway around the world, we were relieved that we could have something elegant for our wedding. It was super specific and kind of silly in the grand scheme of things, but it mattered to us. And we've seen the same level of satisfaction echoed by our customers for years now.

Launching your first product should not be an attempt at revolutionizing your industry. You don't need some big idea for a product that will change the world. You just need something that sells consistently over time in predictable ways. Remember: Growing too fast is not all it's cracked up to be. And growing too slow can easily kill you. So we're looking for that sweet spot between "enough people care about this" and "everyone in the world wants this."

When you do this, you become less of a threat to anyone who might want to take you out. Entrepreneurship is a competition, after all, and you're not getting into this game to put a great big target on your back, are you? You want to keep your company as nimble and as anonymous as possible—at least to your competitors—so that you can stick around for a long time. Don't sell a product everyone wants. Pick one that *someone* wants. Someone specific you can easily describe. The more specific, the better.

Our handkerchiefs are the perfect example of this. Demand for the product wasn't enough for a store like Target to want to carry them, but it was perfect for an online store that just wanted to make a few million bucks a year. That may sound like a lot of money, but it's not to big corporations. They don't want to mess with something so trivial that it requires a level of sophistication to run efficiently. It's just not worth it for them. One of the easiest ways to build a profitable business that can go the distance and remain streamlined is to pick a product that larger companies don't care about. The last thing you want is to get in a price war with Amazon or Walmart. Start small and specific, then broaden your reach after that as needed.

GO WHERE DEMAND IS

Before we figure out what to sell, we first need to figure out who's buying. I recommend picking a niche where the value of what you are selling is somewhat ambiguous. If everyone knows what it costs to create your product, then you can only charge so much for it. Anytime you have a product where you can add value to it in some way that is hard to measure or define, then you've got an asset.

A commodity is something anyone can acquire and resell, but a true asset is something you own that increases in value over time and can then be sold for whatever price the market will sustain. This is why information products, like online courses and membership sites, can be such great products. Any form of intellectual property is a win, because the value of the information is subjective. What may be worthless to one person may be worth its weight in gold to another.

The idea here is simple: Anytime you can find a way to create more value in your product that is difficult to objectively measure, do it. This will allow you to charge more and take you out of the endless race to the bottom that is typical of many industries. If you are selling something almost anyone can get their hands on, you've got to stay competitive. The best way to do that is to distinguish yourself from the competition. You don't need to be better, just different. At Bumblebee Linens, our differentiator is personalization, adding a few initials on a handkerchief. This allows us to focus on a unique corner of the market and niche down on customers who are getting married and care a lot about having their initials and wedding date on a hanky. When we were starting out, we paid almost exclusive attention to this group of people, because no one else was. This allowed us to build a strong and profitable business and has allowed us to maintain a strong share of that market.

Amanda Wittenborn makes over $170,000 per month selling party supplies, decorations, and invitations at amandacreation.com. She started as a result of her love for throwing themed parties. The mother of three sons, Amanda has been designing parties since before the days of Pinterest. The very first birthday party she threw for her son when he turned one was a monkey-themed party where she handmade every single invitation with stamps and scrapbook paper. She even convinced her husband to create eight-foot-tall balloon palm trees for the party.

One of her friends convinced her to try to sell her over-the-top party decorations online. Unfortunately, Amanda didn't have a lot of success at first and thought, "No one's ever gonna buy this stuff." Still, she kept exploring other options and opened up an Etsy store. Sure enough, people started buying her products.

Back then, everything Amanda made was a digital download that could be purchased by a customer and downloaded so they could print it out on their own home printer and then assemble whatever the decoration was. As business grew and life got busier, Amanda considered how she could continue to scale her business smartly. She realized that in spite of there being many crafty moms out there who didn't have the time to spend on personalized party supplies but still wanted something that looked handmade, she was encouraged to create a more finished product that was ready to hang right out of the box. No downloads, no printing, cutting, or taping. Everything is ready to go. She sells them on her own website as well as via Amazon, where she specifically caters to moms in a hurry to get already-assembled decorations that look homemade for parties that are right around the corner. That's quite a niche. The narrower you go, the more success you find.

Now, when you're choosing a niche, you want to have a product that appeals to what author Drew Whitman calls the "Life-Force 8." In his book *Cashvertising*, Whitman says that these core desires are "responsible for more sales than all other human wants combined." It would be wise to consider which types of products most people are willing to buy, no matter what. The Life-Force 8 are:

1. Survival, enjoyment of life, life extension
2. Enjoyment of food and beverages
3. Freedom from fear and danger
4. Sex
5. Comfortable living conditions
6. Being superior to others (aka winning)
7. Care and protection of your loved ones
8. Social approval

Any product that allows you to do these things feels like something you can't live without. Or at least, you don't want to. People rarely make purchase decisions rationally. It's all about how you feel. So if it addresses sexual urges, elevates your status, or keeps your friends and family safe, you better believe people are going to have strong feelings about it. Take Dr. Squatch, for example: They sell soap for men but if you look at their commercials, what they are really selling is sex. Remember those old Herbal Essences commercials where they implied the women washing their hair were having an orgasmic experience—or the Old Spice commercial where the guy getting out of the shower is daring the men watching to be stronger and manlier. These are all appeals to the Life-Force 8, and they work very, very well. Everyone gets hung up on finding a niche, whether it's a physical or digital product. But the truth is you can make anything sell as long as you appeal to a person's emotions. The product is less important than the emotions you evoke in a customer. Focus on the feelings, and the sales will come.

FINDING THE RIGHT NICHE FOR YOU

Everything you sell must have a strong value proposition, but you don't have to please everyone. This becomes even easier when you don't aim for the bottom of the market. Ultimately, when you shoot for the top (i.e., the customers with the most money, expecting the greatest value) that means you're competing with fewer players and the rewards are greater. You will get paid more, even if you don't own all of the market. It's a smart bet. This will also mean you'll have fewer customers and be getting paid more for the few customers you do have, which will lead to less work and more money per customer. No downside there.

This approach allows you to focus specifically on your best customers; then later, if you want, you can produce a different product for the masses. Elon Musk did this with Tesla. He started with higher-end, niche products, then went down market to increase his share. It's a smart way to grow: make the most amount of cash up front, then over time offer more affordable products to other segments of the market. If you can, start with the most specific, highest-value product you can think of, then gradually begin expanding over time with more commodity offerings as you try to appeal to larger groups of people. For example, I have a student who sells leatherworking supplies, and he actually sells tools to people in China who knock off big-name bags, like Gucci and such. A friend of mine sells boat anchors. The opportunities to do this are limitless. First, focus on the most niche product you can imagine that has the greatest value proposition.

You can, of course, begin with a wide approach to the market. Just know that's an uphill battle and will be taxing on your human resources and cash. I mean, do you want to go toe-to-toe with Colgate, or a company called . . . Bumblebee Linens? That's what I thought. Niche down for the win.

How, then, do you research niche audiences that never sound obvious until you hear them? I mean, who would have thought to sell leatherworking supplies or wedding handkerchiefs? You don't know until you try. This is where online search tools can be helpful. Whether you realize it or not, there is a universe of resources available to help you start your business the smart way. You don't have to fly blind like we did and just troubleshoot things. There's help available if you know where to look.

One example is the tool Jungle Scout, which scrapes every single Amazon listing and tells you approximately how much revenue each listing makes. You can query this database and search, for example, all products that generate at least three hundred sales per month and make at least $10,000 a month. By taking a look at what sells, you can quickly find a niche for yourself. Oftentimes, when doing this, people will find products they never would have thought of in a million years. Don't make the mistake of trying to take a bunch of shots in the dark in hopes of hitting big on something. You don't need to do that. Your search for the ideal niche can be informed and sophisticated. You may still need to take a little risk at some point, but it'll be an informed risk.

All I'm saying is that there is a lot of data available to you if you know where to look and what to look for. Another tool to use is a website called Ahrefs.com, which allows you to see what people are searching for on Google and how to optimize your website for those searches. Other platforms have similar resources. There's a tool called Terapeak, which allows you to figure out what all the listings for a certain kind of product on eBay are selling for. That way, you know how to set prices so that you aren't underselling or charging more than the market can bear. The point is that regardless of what you're selling or where, you can find a way to optimize your products and services for what people want. Our goal as entrepreneurs isn't so much to find an audience for our product but rather a product for an audience. That's what niching down is: It's looking for a large enough group of people who have a clearly felt need for a certain product or service. Go where the demand is, and don't be surprised if it's not where you think.

When it comes to finding the right niche, there is a delicate balance between selling what people want and finding a product nobody else is selling. On one end of the spectrum, you need to sell something that has sufficient demand. If it's too innovative or brand new, people won't know what to do with it. This is a mistake we see a lot on shows like *Shark Tank* and in many discussions about entrepreneurship. You don't need to reinvent the wheel to start a business; you just need to make it better. If your business concept is too original, it will be confusing and difficult to explain. On the other hand, if the product category is too competitive, meaning too many people want it, then it can be hard to make any money in such a busy space. I can't tell you how many students sign up for my class with a preconceived notion of what they want to sell but after running the numbers and realizing "selling T-shirts" is probably not the best idea, they go for it anyway. Don't do that. Make an informed decision with the data you have, and don't be afraid to pivot if something better comes along. In these early stages, you want to be somewhat nimble and open to changing things up.

Now, I don't want to say that it's impossible to succeed in a highly competitive niche. But it will be much more difficult and your timeline to profitability will be significantly longer than if you were breaking into a less-competitive niche. The audience that you choose for your business is important, because at the end of the day, everything in business comes down to supply-and-demand. If people don't want it, or if too many are offering it, then you have no business.

Picking the right product to sell will make things much easier for you in the long run, so choose wisely here. In fact, I would not even consider launching a product of any kind without running a quantitative analysis of your potential profitability. It's not a guessing game. There's a science behind choosing the right product.

When I use a database like Jungle Scout, what I like to see is that there's an even distribution of revenue across the front page for all sellers on Amazon. There should not be any single seller dominating the market. To quantify competitiveness, I look at the number of reviews. Reviews are a good measure of how mature an Amazon listing is. If the listings on the front page are in the low hundreds, that indicates the product isn't that competitive.

The best students in my class spend a good amount of time carefully researching their niche before they fully commit. This is true for most great entrepreneurs. The myth of accidentally capturing lightning in a bottle is just that—a myth. Thomas Edison famously ran thousands of experiments before finding the most efficient way to create an incandescent light bulb. In fact, he wasn't even the first to the market; he just found a way to create the longest-burning filament.

This is what it means to be an innovator, to find a way to market that is in some way better than your competitors. You don't have to be the best at everything, but you better find something you can be unique at. It'll probably take some time and tweaking, but when you find the right blend of your skills and the needs of the market, you'll know. Find the right niche for you that allows you to serve the most people for the most profit. Then, start selling.

VALIDATE YOUR PRODUCT

Smart entrepreneurs test their products or services before spending a large sum of money mass producing them. Even though most are anxious to jump straight into the implementation phase, the good ones take their time making sure this first step is done correctly, because they know if they skip it, the likely result is disaster. Don't avoid the trial-and-error part in this journey; it could mean the difference between your "Eureka!" moment and utter bankruptcy. Not only that, the best business owners make sure they provide a unique value proposition (i.e., a solution that solves a unique problem) that makes their business stand out among the competition.

This process of validating your product before pushing all your chips to the center of the table can be challenging for many. Some of us want to have all the answers before we begin. Like: *Is this product going to be a winner? Can you guarantee this is going to work? How much time will it take to make six figures?* It's common to want guarantees, but in business—as well as in life—there are no guarantees. You can do all the research you want, but you'll never know whether something is going to sell until you throw it out there and see what sticks.

WORK BACKWARD FROM YOUR CUSTOMER'S FRONT

Noah Kagan was the thirtieth employee at Facebook, then less than a year later he was fired before his stock options vested.

In retrospect, this cost Noah something like a few hundred million dollars, which he says was the greatest lesson he ever learned—painful as it was. In business, just as in life, nothing is set in stone; and anything can change in a moment. In the case of Noah, he had to learn this more than once before he was willing to bet on himself and become an entrepreneur.

After he left Facebook, Noah went to work for Mint.com and quit before any of his stake in that company vested. Again, this cost him millions. Nonetheless, his experience working closely with future billionaires taught him invaluable lessons about business, risk, and entrepreneurship.

After all this, he took sixty dollars of his own money and started a new company called AppSumo.com, a daily deals site that sells discounted tools and resources for entrepreneurs. He did this on the side, investing very little time or money up front, earning a mere $12,000 in his first year. This business, however, was optimized for his lifestyle and one he was willing to grow slowly over time. Today, AppSumo is a 100-million-dollar business, but it started small and scrappy.

Most entrepreneurs tend to work forward, beginning with a problem they can solve and then finding a group of people who want it. But Noah went in the opposite direction, first asking, "Where can I find a large group of customers, then try to sell them something?" This was a big distinction in how he was building his new company, something he calls "working backwards from your customer's front." Most people, he says, create a round peg and start looking for a hole instead of beginning with the hole and finding something that fits. The latter is far easier.

This wasn't Noah's first entrepreneurial venture. He had already wasted thousands of dollars in previous start-ups trying to sell solutions to problems nobody had. This time, he wanted to do it differently. "How do I just solve people's problems and give them solutions they actually want?" he wondered. One day when he was scrolling Reddit.com, Noah noticed how much fellow Redditors love using IMGUR, an image hosting site where users can share videos and photos online. Seeing that IMGUR had a pro account, which allowed users to have an ad-free experience, he decided to contact the company and explore a partnership. His email to the founder simply said:

Hey

I wanted to also check with you on what kind of promo we can do together. What's best for you?

Cheers,
Noah

They exchanged a few emails back and forth, and IMGUR finally said yes to his request to promote their product on Reddit, agreeing to be paid $7 for every Pro version Noah sold at a discount instead of the normal $29. Noah could charge whatever he wanted, collect payment himself, and keep the rest of the profit once he gave IMGUR their cut.

His goal was two hundred sales.

Now, armed with a product that he was pretty sure Redditors would eat up, he just needed to find a way to get it in front of them. To do this, he reached out to the founders of Reddit via email and offered to take them out for breakfast. Over eggs and bacon, he told what he was doing and asked for some free ad spots, and to his surprise, they said yes. No strings attached. All told, this cost Noah something like $26 (because he paid for breakfast). He now had an audience, a product, and a promotion plan. He just needed a way to sell it. So he spent another fifty dollars to hire a web developer in Pakistan who helped him throw together a quick-and-dirty website that allowed him to accept payments via Paypal. This took about a week to build.

A week after that, armed with his free ad spots, Noah started promoting the discounted one-year membership to IMGUR. Initially, he only charged $8 for the one-year discounted subscription to IMGUR, profiting a mere dollar, and then delivered the product manually by sending an email to the customer, thanking them for the business and including instructions on how they could access their membership codes. Also in this email, he asked what other products or services they might be interested in getting at discounted rates. He eventually raised the price to $12.99, sold his two hundred, and just like that AppSumo was born.

After that, he put together a bundle of products on time management and contacted Lifehacker, asking if they would write about it. No promises, they said, but "that sounds really interesting." Noah went to the top products Lifehacker had already written about and created a custom discount bundle where someone could buy the bundle and get all those products at a significant discount. Lifehacker wrote a long article about it, resulting in the next few hundred sales of that bundle, which was priced at $150.

At this point, he knew he was on to something. It wasn't easy and required quite a bit of leg work, but because of how he took these steps, he was building confidence in the business he wanted to grow without putting all his eggs in one basket. Starting up like this takes a lot of energy and attention, but it's the right way to begin. Noah's advice when starting out, which he wrote about in a blog post documenting this whole story, is: "Always be janky in the beginning." At first, what you sell doesn't have to be perfect. You just need to get it out there.

The best entrepreneurs are comfortable with taking action on imperfect information. They are willing to invest a small amount of money in something to see what works. They are willing to take a small leap of faith, using their skills to add value to a niche market that wants what they have to sell. They find a way to offer something unique and interesting that is different from what their competitors are doing. They do this with discipline, making small bets as they go and seeing how they pay off, tweaking things along the way. And then, as they start to see results, they ramp up their efforts and chase what's working. They aren't afraid to be a little messy for the sake of testing an idea. And in the end, it works—not because they had all the answers at the beginning, but because they were willing to try.

You can, in fact, validate a product without investing any money at all. With physical products, you can start with drop shipping. This is where you sell a product but the supplier is responsible for shipping and fulfillment. You only have to pay when an order is made. Another way is through affiliate marketing. By just referring a sale without any risk or support, you can "validate" something you might want to sell. All you have to do is find out what sells and then source your winners.

SMALL TWEAKS FOR THE WIN

When it comes to finding a fortune side bet, you don't have to think of something that's never been done before. Sometimes a small tweak of a product or service can introduce a best-seller to the market.

For example, once I was at Walgreens, walking the aisles looking for some ibuprofen and happened to see a box of Rogaine. Now, I'm not losing my hair, but it just caught my eye. On that shelf, there was a box that said "Rogaine for Women" in a pink package, and next to it was another box that said "Rogaine for Men" in black. I'm no hair doctor, but a quick glance at the back of each box revealed that they were virtually the same product with the exact same ingredients, and a trusty Google search tells me men and women can use these products interchangeably. I imagine hair-loss products started out primarily for men, but then they began experimenting with selling the same product, in a slightly different package for women. And it worked!

Once you find a product that already has a built-in demand, even if you don't make the product, you can pretty easily find a new audience for it. The hard work has already been done—building the product, testing it, etc.—now you just need to sell it. And if it is already selling to one group of people, sometimes a simple tweak is all you need to do to make it relevant to another market.

Take toolboxes, for example. There are pink toolboxes sold on Amazon that sell really well, in some cases better than the men's versions of the same toolbox. I don't know who came up with this idea, but it was ingenious. Lots of people buy toolboxes on Amazon—men and women alike. I don't have to tell you that the pink toolbox is just as effective as the black one. But by creating a pink one targeted specifically at women (and even more specifically, the kind of women and maybe sometimes men who buy pink toolboxes), the makers created a separate product that was a bestseller over any individual listing on Amazon in its category. Because of how they positioned it, they were able to sell the same product to a different niche and end up increasing their total sales across the board. That's brilliant. What an incredibly efficient way to increase sales.

When it comes to figuring out what you want to sell, start with the skills you can monetize. Can you create something of value or take what someone else has made and resell it? Once you find out what people are willing to buy, can you then find the easiest and most profitable way to sell those skills? Why the easiest? Because there's going to be a lot of work that won't be fun, so make this part as effortless as possible. It's easy to find something to sell to an audience. The real trick is finding the people who want what you have to sell, because the right customer isn't always who you think it might be.

Neville Medhora is a well-known copywriter and online marketing teacher, but before he did that he used to sell fingertip lights as part of a rave supply company. That is, they sold products for people covered in body paint dancing under black lights all night long in abandoned warehouses (I've clearly never been to a rave). Later, he discovered that the majority of customers weren't buying these lights for raves. They were plumbers wearing them on their hands so they could easily see under the sink. You never really know who your product is for until you put it out there and see what people do with it.

CHAPTER 6

Start Before You're Ready

M ost people wait too long before doing what they know they need to do in life. I wanted to start my blog for years before I did. What took so long to get started were two concerns: one, I was intimidated to build my own website on WordPress; and two, I thought I hated writing. So I kept stalling until finally the pain of not starting was greater than the discomfort of just doing it. After that, I installed WordPress—and it was surprisingly easy! Two years of waiting, the whole thing took two hours.

The next day, I typed out my first blog post. It turned out to be much easier than I anticipated, and I could even make it fun. My blog posts didn't have to be long and eloquent; they just had to be helpful and direct. I've blogged regularly ever since then with minimal resistance. Once I ditched my doubts, progress followed. Lots of things are like that.

Most people hesitate to start a business because they doubt they have any marketable skills to offer or think they need to conduct years of research to create a viable business plan. None of this is true. Launching a business is easy. The hard part is getting it to run on autopilot with minimal effort or interference needed from you. Many aspiring entrepreneurs delay the first few steps, which are ironically the least risky ones in the whole process. Nobody is ready to begin—ever. You always have to start earlier than you think.

If you struggle with finding the right idea for your business, the best way to move forward is to look at the everyday problems you experience and try to solve them for other people. My friend Albert Lee is an example of this. He wanted to lose weight and discovered it was really difficult to keep track of his calorie consumption from the foods he ate, so he started a nutrition database online called MyFitnessPal (you may have heard of it) which he later sold for over $400 million.

Similarly, when my wife knew she was going to cry like a baby at our wedding but couldn't find a place to buy handkerchiefs, we knew we were on to something. When Greg Mercer had difficulty with his product research on Amazon, he created Jungle Scout for his own personal use and later decided to release it as a product. Often, the best products or services are the ones that you personally need the most. When you create solutions to your own problems, you are betting that other people have those same struggles, and often you're right.

When it comes to solving other people's problems, remember: The simpler the solution, the better! Chris Boerner started selling pill holders online, because she wanted a fashionable way to carry her medicine. Fashionable pill holders, can you imagine? That's almost as silly as selling handkerchiefs online, which is probably why it worked. You are never alone in your needs and desires. If you have a problem, chances are that other people do, too. Learn to scratch your own itch just to get started, and you may be surprised by how many other "weirdos" just like you are out there.

The good thing about running a business online is that it doesn't cost much money to begin, so why not just throw something up and see what happens? This isn't like the old days when you had to take out a huge loan from the bank to start a brick-and-mortar store. Today, you can start a business with a few hundred dollars. There really is no excuse. If you don't succeed, you can tweak your idea or start something else.

My wife and I started our business with $630 and turned it into a six-figure profit in one year. Launching a business these days requires minimal risk with the potential of a huge payout—if you are patient and smart. The expected value calculations are almost always in your favor. So lighten up and experiment! Don't take this stuff so seriously. And this is coming from me—the calculated, non-risk-taking Asian. Think of starting a business as a series of low-risk trials, not a lifetime commitment to one thing. You can always pivot as you go. If you wait until you're ready, you'll never begin.

IT'S NEVER THE RIGHT TIME

One of the biggest excuses I hate hearing from people is that they "don't have enough time" to start a business. If you look at my current lifestyle, I run an online store, a blog, an ecommerce course, a podcast, a YouTube channel, and plan a yearly event, all while helping raise two kids and not missing any major performance or games. And as I've shared before, I do all this in about twenty hours a week. If you think that's intense, I've had guests on my podcast who homeschool seven kids while running multiple six-figure businesses! Balance is a myth, but just because you have a lot going on doesn't mean it should take all your time.

Toni Herrbach, for example, runs a popular blog called thehappy housewife.com, where she's created an incredible resource for women to help them better manage their homes. She also helps run The Sellers Summit with me, which is a conference that caters to ecommerce professionals who want to expand their online businesses. But here's the kicker: This woman has seven kids and homeschools all of them.

My wife and I have plenty of issues parenting only two children, so I seriously can't even imagine doing that with five more. To my surprise, when I met Toni in person, she was down to earth, calm, and composed. In spite of her many responsibilities and the demands on her time, she was very easy to talk to and didn't seem distracted in the least.

Toni has the time and energy to take care of herself in the midst of a busy schedule not because she has an abundance of time, but because she's learned how to use her time well. Every time I look at my inbox and see someone complaining about not having enough time, I tell them Toni's story. You have enough time to do what you need to do. You just need to learn how to use it. If you get off work at six p.m. and eat dinner, that leaves three to four hours a night to put toward your side project. Couple that with free time on the weekends and you can get a serious amount of work done without having to quit anything. Granted, you don't want to do this forever, but a season of hustle is sometimes necessary to get a new business off the ground. It's certainly preferable to betting it all on some risky side hustle, hoping it'll all pay off later.

My point is simply that there is no perfect time to begin. You will never suddenly have a bunch of free time available to spend on whatever passion project feels exciting. Words like "difficult" and "overwhelming" are relative, especially when we are talking about how people spend their time and energy. You don't need to work yourself into the ground or skip self-care to become an entrepreneur. You just need to get your priorities straight.

Don't make me ask how many shows you're watching right now, how much time you spend on your phone each day, or what sports teams you're currently following. I want you to enjoy your life, be present to your family, and have some hobbies, but I also seriously doubt that you have no time to spare. But that's beside the point, anyway. It's not that you don't have enough time, it's just how you choose to spend it. You are clearly spending your time somewhere, and the key to time management is figuring out what you're doing with it. The time to get started is now. You don't need to wait. Just because things aren't going as fast as you'd like doesn't mean you aren't on track to building a business that can go the distance.

In 2008, my good buddy Pat Flynn proposed to his girlfriend, and a month later he was laid off from his job as an architect. He and his fiancée lived with each of their parents until they got married, then moved in with her parents, post-nuptials. Now, there's not much more that can give a man a giant kick in the pants than living with his wife's parents. Pat had a side business helping architects pass their exams but didn't feel ready to be an entrepreneur. Life, however, had other plans.

Nobody starts a business perfectly. We are all reacting to the twists and turns that are thrown our way, doing our best to make the most of them. So many people say they'll start a business someday, when the circumstances are just right. When they're *ready*. The thing is, you're never ready. There's always a reason to delay, an excuse to stall. If you really want to succeed, you're going to have to begin before you feel fully prepared. Especially if your mother-in-law is folding your underwear.

Pat got started, forcing himself into this space sooner than he expected or even wanted. And yet, somehow he figured it out. Now, his "side business" has turned into a whole suite of companies that includes tech advisorship, software, online courses and membership, and innovative physical products. He sets his own hours, has ample time for family and personal hobbies (recently, he's been trying to master the art of fly-fishing), and even works with a number of charities in his free time.

Today he is living life well and doing business right. If Pat can succeed in less-than-ideal circumstances, then you and I can, too. So long as we decide to start now, with whatever tools and resources we have, no matter how unprepared we might feel. There's always something else to do before you're "ready." But stalling only hurts us in the long run.

WHAT IF YOU FAIL?

If you're concerned about failure, you can always consider what your actual worst-case scenario might be. There's nothing wrong with imagining the very worst thing that could happen just so you know what kind of risk you're taking. Most people fail to start because of their fear, not because of reality. Back when my wife and I started our wedding linens shop, we were worried about a lot of things. We were worried about failing. We were worried about being embarrassed in front of our friends if we didn't succeed. We were worried about appearing successful. We were worried about downgrading our lifestyle and not being able to afford a nice house for our family. We were worried that we wouldn't be able to get new jobs if we crashed and burned. And all of this was distracting us from the messy process of moving forward.

To overcome these fears, we played a game called Worst-Case Scenario. The rules were simple: Take a piece of paper and write down all possible negative outcomes, no matter how outlandish they seemed. This forced us to look at the absolute worst thing that could happen to us. Often, the fear of a thing is worse than the thing itself. Although we were legitimately worried about failing, running through the worst-case scenarios helped temper our fears. We balanced our concerns with more realistic scenarios, understanding that tragedy *could* befall us, but it probably wouldn't. And then, of course, there was the best-case scenario, which was what we hoped would happen. We looked at this whole spectrum of potential circumstances and then made the best choices we could. Maybe this is the tactical poker player in me talking, but I just wanted to know the odds. And this helped a lot.

When considering our chances, our thinking went like this:

WORST-CASE SCENARIO: Our business flops and we both continue to work at our day jobs.

REALISTIC SCENARIO: My wife works full-time on the business while my day job supports the family.

BEST-CASE SCENARIO: Our online store takes off big time and we sip margaritas on the beach for the rest of our lives.

By enumerating all of the worst-case scenarios and then contrasting them with what was more realistic, we realized no outcome was absolutely catastrophic. Any failure we might experience, however unlikely, was something we could recover from. Bestselling author and popular podcaster Tim Ferriss calls this "fear setting" and advocates for imagining the worst-case scenarios over pie-in-the-sky thinking that discounts the possibility of hardship. When you're dreaming of your future, you don't want to be so optimistic in your thinking that you miss some legitimate risks that could take you out of the game. Looking at what you fear the most allows you to make a decision without worrying unnecessarily or naively expecting everything to just work out. You want to make the best decision possible with the information you have.

When my wife and I did this, our analysis gave us the courage to pursue building a business. Almost nothing is ever as bad as it seems, and most of your fears are made-up scenarios that will likely never happen. That doesn't mean there aren't legitimate challenges and risks you face; it's just that you rarely ever think about them ahead of time. Write it all out on paper so that you can clearly see what you're dealing with. Spelling it out on paper can reveal not only how unlikely these things are, but the exercise will give you some security in knowing what you'd do if they did happen.

Let me say it again: You have everything you need to begin. You are good enough. Just start somewhere, anywhere. And if you need ideas, begin by scratching your own itch. You don't have to be super passionate about what you create; you just have to be interested enough to take a small step forward. In all likelihood, you don't have as much to lose as you might think.

CHAPTER 7

Your First $1,000

A VALIDATION PLAYBOOK

To be a good business owner, you don't need a huge marketing campaign or media appearance. What makes a business work is sales, plain and simple—and not millions of dollars or some big IPO. You need cash to come in the door each and every day. And to make that shift from nothing to something makes all the difference for a fledgling enterprise. Once you get that first sale, though, everything changes. So far in this book, we've been talking about the principles behind a family-first business and how to get off the ground the right way. We've also talked about the benefit of starting small, focusing on an underserved niche that you can capitalize on immediately, and why the way to get bigger is usually by thinking smaller. Now we want to move beyond concepts and get to brass tacks. It's time to go from zero to one.

What's the difference between a passion project and an actual business? One dollar. That's all. And that's everything. One simple sale that, with the right effort and focus, will be the first of many. How, then, do you place your fortune side bet and start making real money? To start selling, you've got to do a few things right, but this isn't as complicated as some people make it. The sooner you start bringing in money, the sooner you have a real business. And until you do that, all you've got is an idea. Ideas are great, but cash is better. Instead of jumping at the first business idea you have, try to take your time ensuring the product will sell and that there's sufficient demand for it. The goal in the beginning isn't to grow so quickly that you can't keep up; it's to start making steady sales.

A great goal to begin with is $1,000 in ninety days. Any fledgling business can make that relatively quickly, and once you've done it, you've demonstrated demand. That's what we learned from Noah Kagan's story earlier. All the money and effort in the world can't make an unsellable product successful, but once you find a way to get people to buy something, all you need to do is repeat what you've already done. After you've validated your product, you now have a real company that you can grow to six or seven figures and beyond given enough time, effort, and focus.

Whenever I am asked advice on how to start a business, the same questions almost always arise:

How can I make money fast? I need cash now!
How quickly can I expect to make real money with my business?
What's the best business model to make money quickly?

Now, your definition of "fast" may be different from theirs, but the general consensus is that making money within thirty to ninety days is pretty darn quick. If I were to start all over from scratch, without an audience, without any connections and any businesses at all, how would I make $1,000 as quickly as possible? I wrote out a game plan and have shared it many times with people, and it's proved to be helpful over and over again. In this chapter, I'll show you how to make a quick $1,000 so you can test your next business idea and hopefully validate your first (or next) product. This works if you need cash quickly, but it's also just the smart way to start any business and how I begin every new project.

This is not a process to making a thousand dollars doing random odd jobs. For example, if you do a quick search on the Internet for "how to make money fast" or "I need money now," you'll see a bunch of articles telling how you can make a few bucks here and there delivering food or driving for a rideshare app. They might even encourage you to donate your own blood, sperm, or eggs. That's not what I'm talking about here. These money-making schemes aren't sustainable. You aren't building anything of value, and it's not a good use of your time. If you want to make $1,000 fast using a method that can be scaled into a real business with the potential to replace your day-job income, this is how you do it.

I've walked thousands of entrepreneurs through this process over the years. It's easy, fast, and simple. But it's not just the easy grand that's the win; it's that you can keep going. Whether you need the money or not, doing an exercise like this will give you great feedback on how solid your business idea is and how sustainable it might be. This step is called "validation," and when we stress-test our business with a clear and measurable goal, we force ourselves to get serious. So, let's get into it.

STEP 1: IDENTIFY YOUR MOST VALUABLE SKILLS & THE PROBLEMS THEY SOLVE

What are you good at? To get someone to pay you money, you have to provide value. The first step in this process, then, is to figure out what your inherent advantages are. What is it that you are excellent at? What do you know more about than most people? And how can you provide a product that someone is willing to pay for? What can you teach someone that will improve their life?

Most people get hung up on this step, because they don't believe they are an expert in any given topic. But that's the wrong mindset. If you have extensive experience in a specific topic, you will understand the common problems people face in that same area. And with this knowledge, you can sell a solution—whether that be a physical product, service, or something else.

For example, I've played Ultimate Frisbee for the past twenty-five years, and a common problem players face is that their hands get cold when playing at night. The obvious solution to this problem, of course, is off-the-shelf gloves, but these are usually too thick. You end up losing the feel of the disc, and it just doesn't work. As a result, most players just grin and bear it while their hands slowly go numb. If I really wanted, I could develop my own line of Ultimate Frisbee gloves, but alas, I'm stuck here writing this book. Someone really should do that, though. Anyway, you get the idea—the best business concepts are usually really simple solutions to daily problems you see all around you.

You can also sell your knowledge. As long as you know significantly more than the person you are teaching or providing value to, then your level of knowledge is sufficient. You don't need to be the foremost expert on a given topic. You just need to be expert enough to get it done. For example, I don't pretend to know everything about selling online and I'm sure there are nine-figure ecommerce business owners out there who know more than I do, but my strength is that I'm a good communicator. I can clearly and effectively convey ecommerce concepts to my students and teach them how to start an online business. Do I have all of the answers? Absolutely not. But I possess more than "enough" knowledge to teach others how to do what I've done.

Let's pretend I don't currently run an online business or have any existing assets from my companies. That said, I still have some talents up my sleeve. A few topics I personally feel "expert enough" to provide value on are the following:

- Computer programming and equipment
- Blogging
- Basic web design
- Photoshop basics
- Volleyball
- Ultimate Frisbee
- Podcasting
- Selling online

Am I the de facto expert in any of these topics? Do I have any credentials that justify teaching a course on any of these subjects? Heck no! But I can say that I know a lot more than the average person about these things and could provide tremendous value on these topics for most people. And that's all an expert really is: someone who knows more than most people about a given topic. You don't have to know everything; you just need to know enough to help someone else. Sometimes, when figuring out which problem you want to solve, it helps to think about the problems you've already experienced in your daily life. For example, as a father of two young children, here are some products and services that I've been looking for:

- **SELF-SERVICE COLLEGE CONSULTING:** I want my kids to take the right classes to get into a good school. Hiring a college consultant is prohibitively expensive, but I still want the best for my kids. Having some sort of service that allows kids to do this for themselves so they can adequately prepare for college (at a cost that is reasonable for those who aren't ridiculously wealthy) would be a huge win.

- **PEP TALK FOR KIDS SERVICE:** My kids are still young but old enough now that they rarely listen to me these days. If I tell them something—and pardon the old-man expression here—it goes in one ear and out the other. If there were a service I could pay for, and it connected authority figures to my children via Zoom instead of me nagging them all the time, I'd gladly pay for it.

- **VOLLEYBALL SETTING MACHINE:** My daughter is really into volleyball, and I often attend her practice sessions to set for her. Most other sports, like baseball and basketball, have a machine that will pitch or serve balls, but as far as I know, there isn't a similar machine on the market for volleyball. And I would gladly pay for one, because my wrists are starting to hurt.

- **NEIGHBORHOOD RECYCLING SERVICE:** My kids drink a lot of canned drinks. While we recycle the empty cans, we don't send them back to get the $0.05 redemption per can. We are frugal people but not that frugal. Someone could start a service to collect cans from the neighborhood and split the profits fifty-fifty with households that participate in it. Who would say no to that?

- **APOCALYPSE CONSULTANT:** With an ever-increasing amount of California wildfires and earthquakes (which are a very real threat to our safety), my wife is legitimately paranoid about the end of the world—or at least, of our world. I would gladly pay for a service to help me prepare for disaster just in case the worst actually happens. It'd be valuable to me to provide some comfort to her, as well.
- **PLANT KENNEL:** Recently, I went on vacation to Florida, and most of my plants died. If there was a place to drop off plants when we're on vacation, I'd gladly sign up for that.

You get the idea. These are just examples of needs I noticed in my life today. Now, it's your turn. Come up with a list of problems you have on a daily or weekly basis that you would gladly pay to solve. Then, take a beat and consider any skills that you are good at now. What everyday ordinary problems does someone else have that you could easily solve? You might have to ask a friend or your spouse, maybe ask a few people on social media. But inevitably, you'll find something simple for you that feels complicated and burdensome to someone else.

It's true what serial entrepreneur and founder of CDBaby Derek Sivers once said: "What's obvious to you is amazing to others." Find something that's obvious to you that is amazing to someone else, write down as many of these as you can think of (no matter how random they may seem), and circle the ones that feel most exciting or interesting to you.

One of my friends devours business books in his spare time, so he decided to summarize his favorite books into a *Cliff's Notes* type publication with which he now makes seven figures selling online. Another friend is a professional illustrator who decided to teach a drawing class and now makes six figures a year doing this. Do not discount any talent or random skill that you possess. Write down everything that comes to mind, even if you don't think people will pay for it. You never know what might end up being useful or valuable.

STEP 2: FIND AN AUDIENCE WHO NEEDS YOUR PRODUCT OR SERVICE

Let's say I picked something from my list and chose to teach others how to use Photoshop. Once you know the skill that you want to share, the next step is to figure out what aspect of your skill other people might want to pay for. Ask yourself, if you were to teach your skill to a specific audience, what benefit would they get out of it? Using Photoshop as my example, I wrote down the following ideas:

- Learn how to use Photoshop to make high-converting images for Amazon sellers.
- Learn how to use Photoshop to create Pinterest-worthy photos for bloggers.
- Learn how to use Photoshop to reach any top influencer.
- Learn how to use Photoshop to create product infographics for ecommerce store owners.

Once you have created a list of benefits, think about who might be interested in learning from you. From experience, I know that Amazon requires all main product photos to have a white background. In addition, Amazon sellers often pay a couple dollars per photo to have their images processed by a professional. As a result, Amazon sellers would be a perfect group to market my Photoshop skill set to.

So now that I know who to sell to, I just need to find them. How can you find out where Amazon sellers hang out? A simple Facebook search reveals a multitude of Amazon groups I can target, including one called "Amazon FBA Rockstars." The customers you are searching for, whoever they may be, are out there. It's up to *you* to find them. All you have to do is make a list of potential groups you can market to, then contact them. If you wanted to sell Ultimate Frisbee gloves, you would look for Facebook groups or online forums full of Ultimate Frisbee players. From playing for the past two decades, I know there are plenty of popular blogs around this subject, as there are for almost any niche interest. Your audience is out there; you just have to start looking for them. They're waiting.

STEP 3: START AN EMAIL LIST

Once you have a product or service in mind and a group of people you want to target, sign up for an email marketing provider. An email marketing provider is online software that allows you to gather contact information about your potential customers and easily send messages to them. If you are on a tight budget, you can sign up for plenty of free tools that offer accounts that allow you to add hundreds to sometimes a couple thousand contacts.

Once you've signed up, you'll want to create a quick and dirty landing page that is hosted by your email provider. A landing page is a simple, clear website that you send people directly to with a single goal in mind. In this case, the goal is to provide an enticing offer so you can get a potential customer's email address. Don't make this too complicated. Create something simple and easy that doesn't require a lot of planning or design. It doesn't need to be perfect. You're just trying to generate leads for your business that you can hopefully convert into customers.

STEP 4: CREATE A PROTOTYPE

After you have chosen a skill to market and have an email marketing landing page set up, it's time to create a prototype. If you're selling physical products, this might be a sample of your product that you create to give away or share in hopes of seeing what resonates with potential customers. Back when we first started selling hankies, I used to post in the wedding forums to get ideas and feedback on what we were creating. If you are selling information, however, you can record a tutorial.

Your tutorial should showcase your skills, establish yourself as an authority, and entice potential customers to sign up for your list. Right now, the simplest and cheapest way to share a video is by hosting it on a free hosting site like YouTube, Vimeo, or Facebook. In the case of my Photoshop expertise example, I would create a detailed tutorial video on how to place a product on a white background for Amazon sellers and upload it to YouTube. Lots of people tend to search YouTube for tutorial-type videos, so I figure that I could find a good niche market there.

If you are on a tight budget, you can create videos for free using a service called Loom. Windows and Apple both have built-in screencasting software that you can use, as well. There's always a tool. Your best bet is to Google "free screencast software," and you should be able to find a number of recording solutions. Personally, I use a program called Camtasia to record all my screencast videos, but there are plenty of options available and new ones every day.

Regardless of what software you use, you'll want to mention in your video that people can receive additional free tutorials by signing up for your email list. Link to your email landing page in your video description and display the link at the bottom of the video. The primary goal of this step is to find a simple way to impress people who are watching the video and get them to sign up for your list. You're not trying to become a YouTube star here; you're just trying to get your expertise in front of others who need it and earn their trust and permission to keep talking to them.

This strategy applies to selling physical products, as well. Erick Strider wanted to sell custom-designed opossum pins (yes, you really can sell anything online). She went on opossum Facebook groups (and yes, these actually exist) to see if anyone liked her opossum drawings. She didn't try to sell anything. She just solicited opinions from a group of people who would clearly have an opinion about such things. You don't always want feedback from just anybody, but the right information from the right person is essential when trying to solve a problem. When everyone jumped at Erick's designs, she mentioned that she makes pins over on her Etsy store at Opposum Rot Studio. It was an easy sell. She didn't have to convince anyone of anything. They were already fans of the subject and the drawings. All she had to do was let them know that she had a product for sale.

Today, Erick makes over $1,000 per month with her store. And she was only sixteen years old when she started. It doesn't take a genius, or even a grown-up, to do this. Everyone has a skill they can teach or a product they can sell, and you don't need to be an expert to add value to another human. Take some time to compile your knowledge into a cohesive structure and build a following today so that you can start scaling your business tomorrow.

STEP 5: START MARKETING YOUR PROTOTYPE

Once you have your video and landing page ready to go, the next step is to gather email subscribers. Where do you go to find people who can start following and subscribing to your content? Go where people already are. If you had just moved into a new home and wanted to throw a party in your neighborhood, you'd have to first go out and meet the neighbors, right? If you just hung some balloons outside and waited for folks to show up, that wouldn't work very well, would it? Of course not. You've got to go where people are already hanging out and find ways to attract them back to "your place," which is your website and email list.

Remember when I talked about listening on forum and online group chats to see what needs people have to help you identify a niche worth monetizing? It's time to go back to those groups and see if you can get some of those people on your email list. Armed with a list of relevant forums and groups, you need to post your tutorial to interested parties.

Before you start randomly posting content in places where people have never heard of you, you first need to familiarize yourself with the group. Know what the guidelines are so that you don't get kicked out. Prior to posting a video, ingratiate yourself to the community. Spend a few weeks leaving comments, answering questions, and adding value to the group however you can. Become a part of the community, and make your name one people would recognize. You have to be known before you can be trusted, and joining other communities is one way to bridge the gap between anonymity and trust.

Once you've established yourself as a helpful member of a community, you can then post a video tutorial to the group, something that would be relevant and useful to other members of the group. Returning to my faux case study, here's a sample of what I might write:

Hey everyone! I really love this group and want to give back to the community. If you're tired of paying a company to put your products on a white background, I put together a quick and dirty video that will teach you how you can do this yourself for free. Check it out!

If it's a physical product like Ultimate Frisbee gloves, you might write the following:

Hey everyone! Check out these gloves I stitched by hand to keep my hands warm at night. It's just a prototype but I have a great feel of the disc and my hands are nice and toasty. What do you guys use?

Notice I didn't ask them to do anything for me. I didn't post an irrelevant article or ask them to sign up for anything. I just shared a piece of content that will hopefully engage the audience. Once that happens, I can share with them more information. For the video tutorial example, I might mention that once they watch the video, there is a sign-up link within the video to get on my email list so they can learn more from me about this sort of thing.

For the physical product, depending on the response, I might say something like, "If any of you guys want one, I have some extras. Just put your email down on this list and I'll get back to you." The point is, we want to engage an audience that doesn't know us before immediately moving to the sale. Seth Godin called this form of outreach "permission marketing," which turns "strangers into friends and friends into customers." In his landmark book published many years ago, Seth explained that taking your time with acquiring a customer, honoring their trust and permission, builds an invaluable relationship with an exponential lifetime value of the customer. In short, greed doesn't pay nearly as well as generosity. "Creating value through interaction," he writes, "is far more important than solving a consumer's problem in thirty seconds."

The good news about this approach is that if people don't watch the video or if my gloves-sharing post doesn't connect with anyone, I haven't blown my chance at posting something later that could convert better. In my experience, though, this works well for most people. Create useful content, share it with relevant groups that you are already a part of, then include a link to some form of deeper connection with you and your business. This is permission marketing at its best. Engage people with something useful, ask them to opt in to a list for more, then rinse and repeat.

STEP 6: CREATE A PRODUCT YOU CAN CHARGE MONEY FOR

If you do Step 5 enough times, you should have a decent-sized email list of potential buyers. It doesn't take a lot of followers to make $1,000. All you need are a handful of true fans who are willing to pay you for your knowledge or the problem you solve. I'd recommend shooting for 100 legitimate subscribers (not spam bots or your grandma—unless G-ma is ready to throw down some cold, hard cash). If you're selling information, you should never be afraid of giving too much information away in these tutorials. After all, the better your material is, the more people will want to learn from you.

If you're selling a physical product, all you need is a sample you can sell. It's almost impossible to be too generous at this stage. You're building trust with people, going from anonymity to familiarity; so, within the bounds of the law and your own ethics, do whatever you can to get in front of the right people. The worst thing that could happen at this point is not failure but indifference.

In any case, once you have built a small following, it's time to create a flagship course or physical product that you can sell to your audience. Using the Photoshop example, I would charge something like $300 for an online course that offers step-by-step instructions and full email support. Your price point will depend on your audience, and I happen to know this is a fair price for such a product.

If you end up doing a course, don't record all your material ahead of time. Designing an online course can be intimidating and even more so when you think you have to get it all done before launching. Don't do that. It's just more stress and gives you another reason to stall. In fact, you can customize your course based on live customer feedback while you build it.

The same applies to physical products. Don't spend years trying to design the perfect product. Instead, sell something someone else has already created, learn what people want and don't want, and innovate from there. You don't need to build something before you sell it. In fact, figuring out what sells should inform what you build.

This is exactly how I launched my Create a Profitable Online Store Course back in 2011. I literally sold my class with zero content prepared ahead of time, and it worked like a charm. This accomplishes a few things for you: First, it gives you the peace of mind that you have one less thing to do (for now); and second, it builds more trust with your audience and gives them a chance to offer you feedback as you build it, assuring that the product you're creating will be something your target audience will actually want. It's like getting paid to do market research, except the people helping you with the research are also customers.

If you want to get into the online course-creation space, there are lots of tools and software solutions that make this pretty easy. You used to have to build out a whole separate site, linking together various apps and tools, holding it all together with duct tape. Now you can upload a video directly to a site and it's good to go in minutes! Some tools even have a free plan where they simply take a percentage of the sales as part of their payment. When starting out, this can be a great option, because it minimizes your start-up costs and overhead. You can start growing your business immediately, earning the capital you might need to reinvest in better tools for your business.

That said, you don't need to create a course to teach your skill. If you don't want to build a whole course, you can simply offer your services as a freelancer, coach, or consultant. People can hire you directly to teach them how to do what they need help with. In the case of my Photoshop skill, all I need is four people willing to pay me $250 to make my $1,000. Then, from there, I can raise my rates or find ways to scale the coaching beyond trading time for money. To accept payment for a service, all you need is a PayPal account, and you can use a calendar scheduling tool like Calend.ly to book the sessions. In fact, some of these scheduling tools even allow you to charge the customer directly to book the appointment; that way, you don't have to worry about managing multiple tools.

STEP 7: LAUNCH YOUR PRODUCT

At this point, you should have all of the pieces in place to grow your business and make your first $1,000 fast. You have an email list of people interested in your product or offering. You have the framework for a flagship course, service, or physical product. You have a small library of tutorials or sample products in your tool belt available to promote your brand and build an audience. Now what? Now, it's time to start making money.

If you sell a physical product, all you have to do is email your list a special offer to buy at a discount within a limited time period. For example, let's say you sign up for my Ultimate Frisbee newsletter, and as a thank-you, I promise a 15 percent discount to my store for any new subscribers. With this discount, you can buy anything in the store for a discounted price for the next week.

For information products, like courses and paid tutorials, the best way to sell your product is by giving a live webinar. If giving a presentation sounds intimidating, keep in mind that a webinar is just a fancy term for a tutorial with an offer. Just like all of the other videos you have provided up till this point, you are just creating another tutorial with an offer to buy at the end. It's that simple. Still, people get freaked out about words like "webinar," worrying that they've got to develop a fancy slide deck or get a thousand pieces of software to work together. You don't need to do that.

All you need is a webcam (most modern computers come with them built-in), a microphone (again, this is usually included on even a laptop or just about any set of headphones), and a way to host the webinar. As I mentioned before, I like using YouTube Live because it's free. Another way to sell is to simply work your way into a number of Facebook groups and then ask for opinions about something you are designing. There are a number of options; nobody cares what tech you use as long as it works. It's the material that matters.

So, let's get into the presentation itself. The following is my script for a webinar that works, but this would apply to any kind of presentation, live or virtual.

First, start with an introduction of yourself and your experience in how you solved your own problem using the skill you are going to share with your audience. Spend no more than three to five minutes on this. Keep it short, practical, and clear. We don't need your life's story, just a simple intro and a little context. Nobody cares who your third-grade teacher was, so just cool it with the back story.

Next, provide a detailed step-by-step tutorial and teach like crazy. Do not hold anything back. The better your tutorial, the more likely you will generate sales. It doesn't have to be super-long: Fifteen to forty minutes is a typical length for the teaching section. Beyond that, people start to drop off and miss the opportunity to hear your offer.

After your teaching, present a discounted offer for your course, service, or product to attendees. This offer needs to be time-sensitive. Creating a sense of urgency will entice people to sign up now, and one of the main reasons people don't buy something is they think there's a better time to buy later. Lack of urgency leads to lack of sales. As part of this pitch, provide testimonials for your work so that people know you're the real deal. These don't have to be paying customers at this point, because theoretically you don't have any. Still, people feel better about buying things other people are buying. What you can do is grab some screenshots of comments on groups where you've posted tutorials and use these as social proof for the value you offer people. It's that simple!

Toward the end of the presentation, remind people of the offer, where and how they can buy the product (be sure to include a link), and the limited-time discount. This may feel repetitive to you, but don't overlook the importance of making sure people know exactly what you're selling, how they can get it, and why they shouldn't wait. That said, you don't have to push the urgency button too hard; people understand when there is a legitimate reason to buy now. If you say you are going to raise your price, do it. If you tell people the offer is going to go away at any minute, make sure it does. Authentic urgency moves people. Inauthentic urgency is just annoying and untrustworthy.

As I mentioned, this can apply to any kind of live presentation, but what's cool about a webinar is that it does not require any money, and you can do it from your own home. I currently run monthly webinars using free software and love this approach to selling online. It's profitable, easy, and can be a ton of fun. I love teaching and sharing, and a webinar is an easy way to put your expertise in front of other people and continue to build trust with your audience. Even if people don't buy from you, they will likely leave the presentation (if it was helpful and informative) with a greater sense of confidence in you. They'll just plain like you more.

Webinars are one of my favorite tools for getting people to buy stuff, because they are inherently generous, basically free (other than your time), and people only come if they want to. Based on my understanding of industry norms, the average attendance rate is about a third of your sign-ups. The average conversion rate of live attendees is between 5 and 15 percent depending on your offer and presentation skills.

Let's do some math! To make over $1,000, you need about four sales if you charge $300 per course. If you assume a 10 percent conversion rate and a 20 percent open rate on your email, that means you need about two hundred people on your email list. That's not bad. Now you know exactly how many subscribers you need before you can do your first webinar.

You can now go back to the first few steps and repeat them until you have at least two hundred people on your email list before launching your first webinar. What's great about this process is that it's iterative. You can keep trying and tweaking, learning what works as you go until you find the right blend of teaching, audience, and what to offer.

This stuff works, and you don't have to take my word for it. I've seen it happen again and again, and this book is full of people's stories who have done exactly this, in one form or another, and it really is possible to get paid to share your skill with the world . . . if you can find a way to connect those skills to the legitimate needs of others.

Now, you may be thinking at this point, "This sounds like a ton of work! I don't know if I want to do this for a measly thousand bucks. Will it really be worth my investment of time? Maybe I should just drive Uber, instead." I get it. This is start-up phase stuff, and it's not for the lighthearted. But here's the thing: Not only will this strategy make you $1,000 in the next ninety days, but once you get all these pieces in place, you can keep replicating the strategy to bring in more money over time. In fact, if you keep growing your email list, keep sharing your expertise online, and start teaching monthly webinars, there's a good chance this will lead to a sustainable business that, in time, could lead to six figures and beyond.

I've seen students use this strategy to go from making nothing online to easily generating one to three thousand dollars a month. Remember Arree Chung? He got started by following this exact strategy and made $4,316 in a single webinar with an email list of only eighty people. He had no website and no audience before he started; today, he runs a six-figure business teaching others how to publish their own picture books.

BEYOND YOUR FIRST $1,000

Of course, your first $1,000 is just the beginning. Once you've done this, you have adequately validated your product or service, and now it's time to grow. To efficiently scale beyond $1,000 on autopilot, here's how I would apply the family-first approach to the Photoshop scenario we already explored. First, I would continue to create free Photoshop content for YouTube on a weekly basis. Creating videos on YouTube is like a stock that can only rise in value over time. As you expand your content portfolio, more people will organically find your content and actively seek you out. The more you invest in this strategy, the higher the returns.

Then, I would create a free mini-course that teaches a valuable Photoshop skill. For example, I could take the live presentation I gave in my webinar and use it as a lead magnet (i.e., a free offer that people get in exchange for their email address) to grow my list. After that, I could then create a multi-part email series (that can automatically be dripped out over time) that further demonstrates my Photoshop knowledge. This uses automated technology called "drip sequences" that you can use to send messages to subscribers in a systematic order no matter when they sign up. It's always the same, consistent process. Most popular email marketing platforms make this possible. At the end of that automated sequence, I can then include an offer to sign up for a full-blown paid class. By posting a link to my lead magnet on my YouTube videos, I am able to consistently drive people to this email list and start generating sales on autopilot.

For the Frisbee gloves example, I would continue to create content around Ultimate Frisbee to attract an audience. Then I would release more Ultimate products (other than the gloves) and cross-sell them. To build community, I would run my own Ultimate tournaments or sponsor existing ones. Man, this is a good idea. I should stop writing this book and go build that.

Bestselling author Jim Collins calls this your "flywheel" and credits the success of most exceptional companies to this simple concept. A flywheel is a simple activity done well, over and over, until you create a culture of excellence. "For a truly great company," he writes in the business classic *Good to Great,* "the Big Thing is never any specific line of business or product or idea or invention. The Big Thing is your underlying flywheel architecture, properly conceived."

For McDonald's, their flywheel is getting you a tasty burger quickly. Pixar's flywheel is releasing a predictably great movie every single year, following a particular formula. For you, it's probably something different. A flywheel is simple in terms of what the customer experiences but often incredibly complicated on the back end. It takes a little time to get off the ground, but once your flywheel starts spinning, it doesn't easily slow down. You can leverage this momentum to create all kinds of success.

In the case of my blog over at MyWifeQuitHerJob.com, my flywheel is delivering content to my audience in easy, automated ways. To deliver the course content automatically (i.e., fulfill my orders), I use an online course platform to host all the content and lock it for paying customers. To answer questions across different channels, I use a help desk tool to automate the response of common questions and efficiently monitor all the correspondence with potential and paying customers without being pulled in a million different directions.

I've followed this model with my own online course and have made millions of dollars with only one contract virtual assistant based in the Philippines. Many of my students have done the same. This is not necessarily hard to do; it just takes the right effort applied in the right way.

Most entrepreneurs sit around waiting for some genius idea instead of finding a group of people who want something, then delivering that to them. Once you've validated your product, you have a real business. Up until this point, we've been pretty scrappy with our approach, and that's on purpose. But to truly benefit from the family-first approach, you have to start scaling your effort and time. And this is where things get a little more complicated. Getting the business off the ground is one thing. Getting it to a place where it can run itself is another. Now that we've started, let's talk about sustaining it.

PART II

SUSTAINING

CHAPTER 8

Systems, Workflows, and Automations

All great companies run on great systems. There is no other way to stay ahead in the game of business. But most entrepreneurs start out all hustle and muscle, using brute force to build the business without considering the long-term effects of such habits. We were no different.

At the very beginning, Bumblebee Linens operated almost entirely on "manual" mode. This is common. You don't know what you don't know when you're just beginning, so you try to handle it all in house with as much elbow grease as possible. That's not necessarily a bad thing. It teaches you the ins and outs of your company and forces you to get acquainted with every part of your business. But with this approach to entrepreneurship, my wife and I soon found ourselves at the end of our rope.

Wanting to keep our expenses low and margins high, we opted to do most of the work ourselves. When it came to customer acquisition, we posted in wedding forums to drum up new business. When shipping packages to customers, we manually drove them to the post office. When someone's lonely grandma called to ask about a random item in our store and then proceeded to tell us all about how her grandchildren didn't reach out anymore, we listened. None of this was going to work in the long term, and we started to see that. Staying in business is not just a question of effort; it's a matter of systems. You can't just push your way through growth if you want something that runs efficiently without you.

When we started our business, we were smart, hardworking Asian Americans committed to doing what it took to succeed. We were willing to put the hours in to see our dreams come true, but after a few years of doing this, it was clear that hustle was not enough. We had to start working smarter, not just harder.

To make it as a business owner, you need a reliable way of doing the same thing over and over with precision and without reinventing the wheel. You have to document how you do *everything*, so you can hand off tasks to someone else when your time is required elsewhere. You need systems, especially when it comes to customer acquisition and retention.

EFFICIENCY IS LEARNED

As our mom-and-pop store grew, our "work harder, not smarter" modus operandi became unsustainable. We needed solutions that relied on more than a can-do attitude and the ability to pack boxes and drive to the post office once a week. As orders poured in, we couldn't keep up. We needed a way of serving our customers that scaled beyond our own effort.

If you build a business from scratch that requires a tremendous amount of stamina to sustain, the likelihood of that business lasting a long time is low. Eventually, everything is going to come crashing down, and you won't have the energy to sustain the grind over the long haul. That's where we were headed; once we saw the writing on the wall, we took drastic measures, addressing the dysfunctional patterns we had created. Because if we didn't act fast, our business and marriage was set to spiral out of control.

The paranoid part of my brain that anticipates worst-case situations began to run disaster scenarios. What if one of us got sick? What if our hands were mutilated in a horrible accident? What if we got tired of packing so many damn boxes? We needed a way to ship our products more efficiently and a way to take care of our customers that worked for us *and* them. We needed a way to grow our business that allowed us to keep up with the growth and not have a meltdown every other week. We needed to breathe again.

It's popular these days to start a boutique business and pride yourself on a high-touch, "white glove" experience. I love that. Business owners should aspire to give their customers the absolute best. But unfortunately, this often comes with a cost. What you have today is a lot of people launching online stores and lifestyle businesses, because they know how to make pretty things but don't understand the entrepreneurial necessity of creating healthy systems. Inevitably, many of these businesses fail. Why? Because they're inefficient.

Please, don't ever let anyone tell you that an entrepreneur shouldn't be concerned with efficiency. The most important thing you can do, as an owner, is figure out how to run your business with the least number of obstacles. Simplify, optimize, and systematize—that's your goal. This is how you stay in a game that is highly competitive with a high probability of failure. Of course, some companies use efficiency as an excuse to squeeze more money out of their customers and more time out of their employees without ever giving back. But those businesses either don't last very long or end up with bad reputations.

On the other hand, if you are inefficient (i.e., filling out every packing label with a sharpie and fielding daily calls from Grandma), you will also either go out of business or lose a lot of your profits. Think of all the energy and time you are currently wasting on inefficiencies that could be put into growing your business and delivering even greater value to your customers.

Efficiency is not only a smart move for you, it's also in the best interest of your customers. The more efficient you are, the faster you can deliver a good or service to the people who paid for it, which will make them happy. Don't cut corners or compromise quality, but the more efficient you are, the better you can make everything else—as long as you put some of those saved resources back into the business.

When you optimize your workflows, you can make more money that allows you to create more valuable stuff, and that will attract even more customers. Which will, in turn, provide more opportunities to optimize—and on and on it goes. When done right, entrepreneurship incentivizes business owners to do the right thing, and we get rewarded for it!

So, in the name of efficiency, we began exploring our options. How could we solve our fulfillment problem? How could I stop running packages to the post office on the weekends? Could we find something not only better but more scalable?

SYSTEMS, NOT TEAMS

Many of the conveniences in the world that you and I take for granted were invented by people just like us. Most of our old problems are now trivial to solve due to the solutions created by previous generations of human beings. The downside to all this innovation is that as things get easier, people get lazy. Because we don't have to come up with solutions to daily threats to our existence anymore, we don't. And as a result, we forget how ingenious humans can be. To start a business, you must tap back into this natural problem-solving ability. You need to be smarter than the average entrepreneur.

In recent years, I've noticed a disturbing trend among entrepreneurs in the small business community. Many have this idea that when they're trying to build something from scratch they can just get everyone else to do the work. *Scale up, grow fast, hire help to keep up.* That's their motto. But this is not the best approach for a number of reasons. A lot of business owners swear by this approach as the fastest route to growing a business. "Want more money?" they say. "Hire more people!" That's a nice idea in theory, but the reality of getting another person to help you in your business is way more complicated.

There are at least two problems with such an approach. First of all, nothing is more expensive than a bad hire. It may be true that hiring can be one of the fastest ways to grow your company—that is, when it's the right people—but it's also the fastest way to go bankrupt. Second, outsourcing every aspect of your business means not knowing that part of the business yourself. What happens when something in your business breaks and you don't know how to fix it? You don't have to build your business from scratch, but you should be involved in the process, especially early on. You put yourself at great peril when you entrust too much to others who have less of a stake in the success of your company.

I am a huge proponent of relying on computers and human capital to do the heavy lifting for you. This is where entrepreneurship can be fun, when you finally stop having to work so hard and let the systems and automations work for you. But you can't rush to give away all the work to someone else.

Once, one of my students hired a web developer to design her site. This person didn't know anything about content management systems or open-source platforms like WordPress, so every time she needed a small change or update to the site, she had to pay an hourly rate to get her developer to do it. This included even stupid things like adding a link or graphic to an existing piece of content on the website. Then one day when her website went down, her developer went radio silent, and my student was helpless. From that day on, she vowed to learn basic HTML so that if her website ever broke again, she'd be able to fix it. Today she is much more self-sufficient as a result, and her business is doing better than ever.

As an owner, your job is to find ways to maximize the resources you have, the most valuable of which is your time. It can be smart to purchase people's time and other resources and sell them for a higher price. That's Business 101, especially when it comes to any kind of service you provide. But when you're just getting started, be careful with abusing the easy button. You can't outsource everything, at least not at first. This should be done with great care so that you are sure to do it well.

Outsourcing everything is a quick way to get into trouble in business. Because once you give it away, it can be hard to get back.

Of course, there's a time to let go of some of the daily operations and responsibilities, but there's also a time to put your head down and do things yourself until you understand enough to hand off a task to someone else. Far too often, however, I see the former being the only strategy utilized by early entrepreneurs. No wonder so many small businesses fail. Hiring is not your only option, nor is just outsourcing. Instead of building a big team or giving all your work to contractors who won't care as much as you do, focus on creating automated systems.

How do you grow a company efficiently and effectively without taking on the added hassle of managing a team? For us, it was simple: Hire robots over humans. In general, I'm a fan of people. As a dad, I've helped create a couple myself! But people come with a lot of complications, and if you can minimize that drama while launching a company, do it. Once I tasted the sweet joy of automation freedom, I couldn't go back. I wanted to see us optimizing everything everywhere, because it always meant better, more reliable service for our customers, higher profits for us, and more freedom for my family. I was sold.

Whenever you can use robots or computers to do a better job than a human can, it's worth it. That's not to say you shouldn't or won't work with humans; it just means you should only hire them for the jobs they should be doing. If you can easily document a task or process, then find a piece of software to automatically do it without question, complaint, or asking for a raise. That's the best way to solve that problem.

YOU CAN'T AUTOMATE WHAT YOU DON'T UNDERSTAND

Despite my affinity for computers and automated systems that get the work done while you sleep, don't jump in right away. Don't start automating until you've reached a certain threshold of pain. Does this mean you never automate or outsource? Of course not. Creating automated systems and processes is something I nerd out on, but we all should start out manually operating our businesses to understand what we may eventually want to automate.

Learn to make your own dough (literally) before you hire your first junior baker. I mean, if I can learn to sew, you can step more into your business operations and get your hands a little dirty. Otherwise, you may spend a lot of money and time going in a direction that makes your life more complicated.

The reason you don't want to automate everything at the beginning is because you have to fully understand *what* you are automating before you can find a solution *to* automate it. One of the most disastrous choices you could make in your business is to outsource a task that you don't yet fully comprehend. That would be like hiring a babysitter before you learned to change a diaper. I mean, I love a night away from the kids, but some steps simply should not be skipped. The game of business is really a series of experiments that all teach you something, and it takes time to master them.

Not long ago, I had a student who wanted to outsource their advertising. They were still early on in their business and were getting ahead of themselves. Sales and marketing, because they are so integral to the growth of your business, should be the last thing you consider outsourcing. When an entrepreneur rushes to hand the reins for growing their business over to someone else, that never goes well. The classic example of this is Steve Jobs hiring John Scully to run Apple as CEO, Scully and the board ousting Jobs, then driving the company into the ground only to hire the founder back to save the company. With very few exceptions, no one is going to care about your thing as much as you do—especially when it's brand new.

I had another client who tried to automate search engine optimization, and they didn't know anything about SEO. You can't do that. No one can automate a task if they don't know what they're doing in the first place. Ever driven through one of those automatic car washes before? If you don't know how it works—that you've got to put your car in neutral and let the automatic track guide you through the wash—then your car isn't going to get clean. You don't have to be a car-washing genius to understand this, but some basic understanding is required. Same goes for your business. You have to know how to do it yourself first before you choose to automate it—that's my philosophy. Then, once things become painful, look first for solutions that don't involve people.

RULES FOR OUTSOURCING & AUTOMATING

I have a series of rules I follow when it comes to outsourcing and automation. These may seem a little extreme, but the more you can afford to follow them, the more bulletproof your business will be.

RULE #1: NEVER OUTSOURCE ANYTHING THAT HAS TO DO WITH YOUR UNIQUE VALUE PROPOSITION OR CORE COMPETENCY. If one of the value-adds of your business is great customer service, don't outsource it. Always handle mission-critical tasks in-house and don't even think about outsourcing them. This doesn't mean you can't create efficient systems and processes that you then automate; it just means that you aren't blindly letting someone else handle a crucial part of what makes your business unique. To do so would be incredibly foolish and risky.

RULE #2: NEVER OUTSOURCE A TASK YOU DON'T UNDERSTAND. In other words, learn how it works before asking someone else to do it. You don't have to become an expert in everything your company does, but you need to know the basics. Figure things out. Doing something in-house is different from entrusting a contractor to do it and will give you greater insight into what a task is worth and what it takes to actually complete it. I'm not opposed to outsourcing, just don't rush into it without understanding what you are getting into or asking of someone else.

RULE #3: OUTSOURCE TASKS YOU COULD DO YOURSELF BUT DON'T HAVE THE TIME AND INCLINATION TO DO. If you know how to do something already and don't enjoy doing it, then it makes sense to outsource it. Being an entrepreneur is about learning new skills, so part of the reason you take on a task is to learn something. You should always be learning and growing in your business, which means you may change hats as you go. I am often finding new problems to solve, learning how to solve them, then automating the solution so I can free up my time and energy to learn something new. Outsourcing is a way to make more room for what you are best at—or what you are curious about learning next.

Jordan Harbinger, one of the world's top business podcasters, told me that long before he became a dad he understood outsourcing was going to be an important part of his work-life balance. Even as an early entrepreneur, he knew that if he succeeded he would eventually have more opportunity than time. From the get-go, he invested where he could in high-quality talent so he could focus on his areas of genius without getting bogged down by the daily doldrums of running a business.

These little tasks can keep you stuck reacting to surface-level problems instead of digging into the deeper issues of building a business. As a philosophy, Jordan believes in hiring teams and organizations wherever possible and paying top-dollar for the work. "You don't have to outsource to someone in India," he told me. "You can hire a company." Don't get someone who isn't as good as you to do something; get someone better and pay them accordingly so they are committed to whatever you've hired them to do.

RULE #4: DON'T BLINDLY USE THIRD-PARTY SOFTWARE. One of the reasons we want to do something manually before automating and outsourcing it to a piece of software is so that we don't break things. If you are dealing with any kind of technology in your business, this is a must. I've gotten burned a few times installing WordPress plugins (which are third-party software solutions that are supposed to play well with the website-building software WordPress provides) only to discover they were horribly inefficient and full of security issues. I discovered this because I learned to program, looked at the code, and found it was poorly written. Bad code is like a wrench in the gears of your machine; it'll make everything fall apart quickly. Be careful what you let into your business. Everything you don't understand is a liability. Make sure you know what you're bringing in and what you're entrusting to others.

RULE #5: DO AS MUCH "IN HOUSE" AS YOU CAN. Every single aspect of your business that you outsource is a potential point of failure. No one else is going to care about your business more than you do, so it pays to be in control of as much as you can. Even if your business falls flat on its face and fails completely, you'll have the knowledge gained in the process. That is more valuable than you realize.

There's a reason so many millionaires lose all their wealth only to rebuild it in half the time. Once you know how to do something, you can do it again. Each time I start a new project, I enter the playing field with more experience, more skills, and even greater advantage. Don't underestimate how important you are in this equation.

DO THIS BEFORE YOU DIE

If you want to build a company that gives you the freedom you long for, you have to start thinking about systems. You might even have to befriend a robot or two! All organizations, no matter the size, live or die on their ability to take daily, repeatable tasks and systematize them. As we've already established, many people hate doing drudge work. Fortunately, that's no longer necessary. You don't need to put a bunch of people on an assembly line or in a phone center anymore. You can let computers and machines do a lot of the heavy lifting, and save the real genius work for people.

Everything in your business that is tedious needs to be automated. And if you can't automate, try harder. Look around. Make sure you're not just creating more work for yourself than necessary. Most of the stuff I started doing manually in our business was eventually automated, not because someone invented a solution, but because one already existed! I just had to find it, or on occasion create one.

In our business where we do personalization, there was one step where a human literally had to click on our website and cut and paste the personalization to another computer program which was then sent to a sewing machine. I never thought in a million years that there was a way to automate this until I started looking. Ultimately, I found a computer program that will move and click a mouse for you automatically and do the cut and paste. This ended up saving us four hours a day. Sometimes, your most strategic solutions aren't anything fancy or world-shattering. They're just more efficient ways to solve a problem.

Every problem you face is probably not as new as you think; someone somewhere has already dealt with it and already found a way to solve it. Find them, a tool they've created, or someone who already knows. And if you absolutely can't automate it, create a replicable system that anyone can use. Take out all the guesswork so that you can focus on solving other problems.

Wherever possible, work with a machine, not a human. They're more reliable. If you do need to work with people, you must make sure everything is documented so that it can be systematized and, wherever possible, automated. This is the stuff that either sets you up for long-term success or will be the cause of your demise. As author Michael Gerber says in *The E-Myth Revisited,* "The system isn't something you bring to the business. It's something you derive from the process of building the business." Building good systems and workflows for your business can be a little tedious, but the sooner you can do this, the better.

PICK A PACE YOU CAN MAINTAIN

Whenever I start a business or take on any additional task, I make sure that I can maintain a certain pace, whatever it is, forever, without it really affecting my life. When you think of all the tasks you have to perform as a business owner, think about longevity.

Sure, you can pack boxes and answer phones and talk to vendors every single day . . . for a while. But eventually, if it's all on you, you're going to burn out. And that's not a business, that's a job. Rarely is it the case where an entrepreneur is easier on themselves than an ordinary boss would be. At least in a job, you get to go home and not worry about the work until tomorrow. When it's *your* company, you're constantly thinking about tasks not done, problems that still need solving, and systems that haven't been created yet. So try to think carefully about everything you're responsible for and what kind of energy you can bring to it over the long haul.

Make sure you are setting yourself up for long-term success. Wherever possible, make your future job easier, not harder. Don't set a pace that is unsustainable or a level of intensity that you can't maintain for years to come. Automate and systematize as much as possible; create workflows that work for you instead of the other way around. A good system, once set up, should make a job that you have to do today even easier tomorrow. Take email marketing, for example. Personally, I don't like corresponding with people much at all. I know that probably surprised you with all this talk of robots, but it's true. I don't like doing customer service. I don't like drafting separate emails to everyone. I like programs, software, and machines. They do what they're supposed to do every single time. People, on the other hand, are a little unpredictable.

Workflows make your work flow. Corny but true! Everything that's new often starts out fun, but eventually it becomes drudgery like most things. So before I begin anything, I try to consider how to optimize the workflows at the outset. There's no need to start out inefficient if you don't need to!

One example is my podcast. In spite of the fact that it was a popular way a lot of my peers used to promote their work, I was not willing to take on podcasting at all until I had a method for pumping out episodes without me having to do any work outside of just recording. What I did first was spend a lot of time not recording. Sounds silly, but it's actually smart. Most people just jump into an activity without really thinking about what will be required of them, and then they end up with a whole list of obligations they don't know how to manage. That's dumb.

Instead of doing that, I spent a lot of time breaking down the pieces of the tools I needed to produce a good podcast, what the exact procedure was to edit an episode, and how to put all the pieces together, documenting every single step. I figured out exactly how I wanted everything to be edited, doing it first myself to ensure quality, then recorded the entire workflow in Camtasia.

After that, I hired a remote virtual assistant to do all the editing and sent them the videos. It was very smooth, and we've been working together, without any hiccups whatsoever, ever since. In the event that I ever lose my podcast editor, I can just point someone else to the document I've created, and they can pick up right where the last person left off. That's the power of a good, documented workflow. Systems matter. Establishing workflows for your business that allow you to make things easier and more efficient is how you save money and time, and this is everything for the future of a company.

CHAPTER 9

Generating Leads and Traffic

Now that we understand the importance of systems, let's apply these lessons to generating leads for business. Thus far, we've been talking about doing marketing and sales manually: going out and finding people in online forums and places where you can figure out what they want and sell it to them. This only works for so long. After a while, you need to start thinking "smarter" not "harder." The more you can get customers consistently and automatically coming to you, the better.

Every business needs "traffic"—people walking past your shop, visiting your website, checking out what you sell. This is the lifeblood of all growth. Without a steady flow of leads, your businesses will die. And if you constantly have to be chasing new prospects, you will eventually run out of energy. The smart way to get and retain more customers is through a process called "lifecycle marketing," which is the process of engaging with your customers along multiple touchpoints to turn them into lifelong customers.

With lifecycle marketing, you manage communication with your customer throughout their entire experience of interacting with your business. From discovery to interest, to first purchase, to repeat purchases and brand loyalty, you are watching it all. You can use content or ads to attract the customer, then use email and retargeting (via paid ads) to continue exposing them to your brand until they make their first purchase. After that, you keep the lines of communication open with your active customers to get them to buy from you forever—or for as long as they find value in what you're offering.

When it comes to our ecommerce store and blog, I separate lead generation into two categories: long term and immediate. Long term is the stuff you do that takes time to build momentum, but once you have it working for you, they pay dividends for years to come. The downside to long-term lead gen is that while you are building these systems, you will not be making much money in the short term.

On the flip side, immediate lead gen brings in paying customers right away who have high potential value but tend to be more expensive to acquire. You need both. So let's look at each and how to create a steady flow of leads that you can systematize and automate over time.

CONTENT CREATION

One form of generating new leads is through creating content, and lots of it. Once you've published a podcast, video, or article, anyone in the world can find it via search engines. This is a long-term but reliable way of bringing in new leads to your business. It just takes time for the content to get indexed by search engines, increase in rank, and deliver traffic to your website.

Search engine optimization (SEO) typically doesn't really "kick in" until about six months after you publish something, meaning any content you create today won't begin to generate organic traffic until half a year from now. Of course, there are exceptions to this rule, like when a piece of content goes viral, but in general, it's best to assume the worst than expect the best.

For example, it took my YouTube channel two years to gain traction before people started finding me from it. Today I receive hundreds of thousands of prospects every month whether I post a new video or not. Similarly, I've had posts on my blog that are ten years old and still generate thousands of visitors every single month on autopilot. These leads, once properly qualified, can easily be funneled into your products and services and turn strangers into customers. This slow-and-steady approach can become quite powerful, provided you have the patience and cash flow to invest in it.

You always want to be creating content in the background, one way or the other, so that you have a consistent, passive flow of leads to your business. Because once you start creating content and get this system working for you, it keeps going. If you feed the flywheel, it keeps spinning.

The goal with long-term content in general, then, is not just to build traffic, as many bloggers and podcasters do. You aren't trying to get famous here. Not all leads are created equal. Rather, you're trying to find the right people who need what you're offering (once you've validated your product). This isn't just entertainment. You want to create the kind of stuff they would be searching for, the kind of content that would get someone to feel like they know you and could trust you.

Once trust is built, you can lead an audience just about anywhere, so long as it's relevant to them. Content is crucial in earning a customer's trust, because the more you educate and inform them, the more you help people, the more they're going to believe you and want to hear from you. If you can get people to consume your content, you can get them to like and trust you, and if you can get them to like and trust you, you can get them to buy from you.

This is how we get out of the rat race of competing merely on price with our industry peers and really start to establish long-term value with our customers. It's brand-building 101. A brand is not just a logo or a tagline. It represents a consistent way of doing things—a promise to your customer—that people come to rely on. Nike isn't only trying to sell the highest-quality, most affordable shoes for their customers. They're having a conversation with their audience that goes far beyond a swoosh.

Another example would be Amy Porterfield. Today, Amy is one of the top online marketing experts, but her road to a fulfilling life and business was far from smooth. As a self-proclaimed "corporate yes girl," Amy prided herself on coming through for friends and colleagues, even at the expense of her own personal well-being. Since starting her business, teaching others how to build powerful online followings and monetizing them, she has learned the art of balancing work with the rest of life and teaches others to do the same. What people love about her is that even though she is a well-recognized expert in her field, she still comes across as an everyday human, warts and all. She shares her struggles publicly, and people relate to her. Because of this, they trust her. That's what a brand is all about, and great content allows you to be clear on what you're offering.

WHAT ABOUT SOCIAL MEDIA?

When it comes to social media platforms like Facebook and Instagram, I am a fan of using them to build your brand, but the traffic is both unpredictable and short-lived. Content on social media is, of course, content, too. It's just not on a platform you own (i.e., your website, blog, or podcast), so with places like Twitter, Instagram, and Facebook, you're posting these videos, images, and messages on "rented land" and at any time the company that owns the network can shut you down.

The one exception to this rule is YouTube, which is technically not your platform but provides long-term, high-quality leads and tends to reward creators who use it consistently. The more content you post on YouTube, the more it gets indexed, and the easier people find you. The rest of social media is a bit more of a treadmill. When you're running hard, you can keep going fast, but as soon as you slow down a bit, the traffic drops. Unless you plan on going viral (which is almost never planned), social media is not a reliable strategy for generating lots of long-term traffic. Stick with videos, articles, and podcasts for that.

Long-term traffic is relatively low risk and provides a reliable return over time. No big risk, but a huge payoff—eventually. Social media, in contrast, provides a "slot machine" of traffic (sometimes you hit it, often you don't) with the potential to generate huge bursts of unreliable traffic. It's good to have a blend of both, and for you, these channels may look different. But the fact of the matter is that you want to build inbound referral sources so that leads come to you and not the other way around.

Sometimes a tweet or Facebook post can become a piece of high-performing, long-term content. But for the most part, after a few days of publishing, the stuff you share on social media will quickly disappear and people will forget about it. Recently, I had a Twitter post go viral, which generated about 1,600 new email subscribers to my list and over two million impressions in one day. Two days later, it was gone.

I'm not anti–social media marketing; you just need to have the proper expectations. Social media can lead to long-term results, because it helps you build a following that trusts you and listens to you. When done correctly, it can convert cold audiences to paying customers, but it's less reliable for that. The conversion rate is typically lower on social platforms, because people are there to hang out and not necessarily to shop. Social media is primarily a branding effort that allows you to keep showing up for your audience and building trust. In order for it to work, though, you've got to stay on top of it. As with most branding strategies, the goal isn't to generate leads or sales, necessarily, but to build long-term rapport with your audience.

TikTok, in my experience, is the only exception to this rule. Granted, it's still relatively new, but the traffic on TikTok tends to stick longer than that of other social media sites. I spend more time creating videos for TikTok because they have the potential to be long-term content that can generate a steady flow of leads. The goal here is to get people on your bus so they will buy into your way of seeing the world. Then you can build a relationship with them over time so that they trust you and will buy from you. That's the goal of social media in a business marketing context.

You need to balance both social media content and longer-form content, such as blog posts and videos, because both are needed. If you focus too much on social media, you're constantly treading water and feeling like you're on a hamster wheel. If you want your business to grow faster with social media, you must consistently post more frequently. And you either have to put in more hours yourself or invest more money in a sales team.

I'm not a fan of this approach to marketing because it doesn't scale well. You always want to have some sort of long-term and passive means of traffic generation, because over time, this becomes a reliable flow of steady leads. You may not see results until six months to a year later, so it doesn't work in a pinch. But you need to have that going in the background if you want to have a baseline of leads and sales upon which you can build. My blog gets a few hundred leads per day passively, and many of my peers report similar numbers. Building a solid system of referral generation will make it easier to grow your business over time.

When most people are starting out, they get impatient with their business and want to see traffic right away. So they post a large quantity of content on social media in a short period of time and then stop. But that's not how this game is played. You have to put yourself on a content creation schedule. For example, you may publish a new blog post and email newsletter every Monday and notify all your subscribers when you do. Or maybe you are publishing three videos a week on Monday, Wednesday, and Friday. Whatever you do, make sure it's done at a pace you can maintain forever. This is not a short-term thing. You have to be willing to publish content online at a pace that you can maintain for a very long time. It needs to become part of your routine.

Most people don't think like this. They end up chasing fads and trying to go viral, wasting time and money pursuing vague goals, and that's a crapshoot at best. The better way to treat content is as a long-term play that requires patience and perseverance. If you need sales sooner, you should explore other strategies. So let's talk about the other form of lead generation now.

ADS, INFLUENCERS, AND MORE

The most obvious form of reliable, immediate traffic generation is through paid advertising. In most industries, advertising is how you get new customers in the door quickly. It costs money and takes time to learn, but if you know what you're doing, it works.

When first starting a business, I will spend some time and money learning to advertise on a new platform. Each one is different, and what works best in one place doesn't necessarily convert to the next. If the product has search intent, Google tends to work well as an ad platform. For products that are innovative or may require explanation, Facebook and Instagram tend to work better. Depending on what you're selling, you may want to experiment with low-cost ads on a number of platforms. Some ecommerce platforms have advertising options, as well, that may be worth trying out. Plug in directly to a source of leads that, when properly vetted and qualified, will lead to sales.

The issue with paid advertising is that it's someone else's platform—you don't own it—so you have to pay for access. You also need to make sure that the price you pay to get the lead is less than what the lead is worth. So if I'm paying, for example, a dollar for a lead, and on average it takes me ten leads to get one new customer, then to recoup my advertising costs, I need to sell at least a $10 product if I want to break even.

Of course, you can try to play the long game and be willing to acquire customers who have a high life-time value, but without sufficient capital, this strategy will bankrupt you. So, in general, you want the traffic you generate from ads to pay for the cost of the ads, at least when starting out. Really, though, the goal of an ad is to introduce people to your ecosystem and start developing a relationship with new leads and prospects so that you can keep selling them stuff for a long time.

Another immediate form of traffic is relationships with influencers in your industry. Granted, it may take some time to form these relationships, but once they refer business to you, the sales come almost immediately. You don't need to slowly build trust with this form of lead gen. It comes automatically whenever the influencer mentions you or your brand.

When you partner with people who have large audiences and are willing to share your work with their followers, you can get quick sales. If a celebrity or industry leader endorses your work, it means instant trust. You don't have to convince people to buy your product; they're ready to be sold because of how much they trust the person endorsing it. These relationships are key in making a big splash in your niche. Influencers who endorse your product with longer-term forms of content such as blog articles, YouTube videos, or podcast episodes can also lead to long-term residual sales. It's the best of both worlds in many ways.

For most companies, influencers are a source of immediate traffic and sales. However, the right way to do influencer marketing is to build a relationship where the influencer promotes the product on their own volition. For example, I promote many tools because I like the company and the people, not because I'm paid. This strategy works, but it takes time to build quality relationships and because it takes a lot of your time, it can be slow to scale. The influencers who have worked the best for us are the ones with whom I've built a relationship over time. It's not an immediate thing and shouldn't be.

In addition to leveraging influencer marketing, you can also form partnerships with other brands. An example of a partnership for Bumblebee Linens that we made early on in our business was with an online florist who created floral arrangements for weddings around the country. Whenever they would sell flowers to a couple getting married, the florist would tell their new customers, "Hey, there's this place that sells embroidered wedding handkerchiefs in case you're interested!" Likewise, if someone was looking for handkerchiefs at our store, we'd point them to the flower boutique. It worked like a charm. Obviously, you can't do this with your competitors, but you can do it with industry peers where you're serving the customers in unique ways.

Other ways to acquire new customers include running online giveaways where you offer a piece of your product for free to get people on your email list so that you can contact them and sell them something. In the past, we've partnered with other wedding-related companies to create a gigantic giveaway. Every company contributes a gift card to the pot and emails their list about the combined giveaway. Then, at the end, every company keeps the entire email list of entrants. Using this method, we've grown our email list by over ten thousand in a single giveaway with just a $500 gift card.

THE THREE-PRONGED APPROACH TO LEAD GEN

So, there you have it, two approaches for generating leads: long term and immediate. Long term is social media and longer-form content like video, blog posts, and podcasts. And immediate is paid ads and influencer marketing. Let's put it all together now.

In our businesses, we have a three-pronged approach to generating leads.

THE FIRST PRONG IS PAID ADVERTISING. This is easy and quick; it can just get expensive. But when you need cash quickly, advertising is the way to go. For our business, we use Google ads for immediate sales. It works every time. The beauty of Google ads is that the visitor already has purchase intent based on their search query. If someone does a search for "ladies hankies," for example, they are likely ready to buy. The more we focus on relevant searches, the higher our ad conversions will be. If we're in a pinch or launching a new product or we just want to maximize the amount of revenue we're bringing in, we will pay to generate traffic and direct it to an offer that converts. It's a reliable means of lead gen and immediate sales. Don't neglect running paid ads because it's a clear winner. Just know that as soon as you stop spending, the leads stop flowing.

THE SECOND PRONG IS CONTENT. To offset the short-term expense of paying to get leads and the risk of being too beholden to someone else's platform, we also create content to generate longer-term traffic. We have to be patient with this strategy as it takes months for content to rank and start attracting the right kind of customers. But since we've been consistently writing blog posts and filming videos for years, it works quite well for us. Articles and pages I created years ago are still bringing in business every day. For example, we typically rank #1 to #3 on a Google search for the term *Ladies Hankies*. That's from writing blog posts on our website and then linking them to product pages throughout our site—something we did years ago. This stuff takes time. We have a disciplined content creation schedule we stick to every week that keeps our brand top of mind with our customers and prospects. This second prong of content creation is a lot of work and takes significant focus. But it works incredibly well, given enough time.

THE THIRD PRONG IS RELATIONSHIPS. This depends on the industry you're in, of course, but my businesses basically operate in two completely different industries—one is weddings and the other is online marketing—and both of those are incredibly relational industries. Whenever possible, I look to build relationships with my industry peers. Here's how this works with each of our businesses:

With Bumblebee Linens, we try to connect with event planners (i.e., people who would buy from us in bulk and consistently come back for more products) as much as possible. This allows us to generate sales in the short term while also establishing longer-term partnerships and strategies for ongoing lead generation. These people are our customers, but they also refer us to their peers and clients, creating all kinds of long-term lead gen potential.

With MyWifeQuitHerJob.com, I build relationships by going to conferences and networking with other bloggers and podcasters. It works the same way as in the ecommerce business. When you connect to the right people, it helps you generate instant sales and create long-term opportunities for you and your brand. In my case, I use ads to generate immediate leads, social media and digital content to nurture these leads into long-term prospects and strategic relationships and partnerships to multiply my reach and sales. In this way, relationships can satisfy both the immediate and long-term marketing strategies—they're the best of both worlds.

Granted, not all these strategies are automatic, but once you implement them a few times manually, you can make them more efficient. You don't necessarily have to automate everything you do to bring in business. Some things, like relationships, can't ever be totally automated—and that's a good thing. But the fact remains that the more you systematize as many aspects of your business as possible, the easier your life will be.

This is especially true when you solve the problem of bringing in new business. Ads, content, and relationships make the mystery of growing your business more of a science. Figure out what works for you and keep repeating it to watch those numbers grow. Systems rule our businesses and, in many cases, our lives. Learning how to harness them will make everything you do as an entrepreneur easier.

So far, when it comes to systems, we've talked about what it takes to make lead generation and customer acquisition as easy as possible. Now that we have a system for generating new leads every day, we need to create a way to keep our customers and get old leads coming back.

CHAPTER 10

Retention and Return

The only thing harder than getting a customer is keeping one. When we learn the art of retention, we go from treating our business as a gig that generates short-term cash to an asset with long-term value. But most entrepreneurs never take the time to really consider how important staying in touch with their customers is. You don't need to always be marketing if you know how to keep people coming back.

According to a survey conducted by Oberlo.com, the average conversion rate in online marketing for ecommerce businesses is about 2 percent. This means that 98 percent of your potential customers are not buying from you. And if you *do* get them to buy, they will not come back and buy again unless you remind them. Most customers find your store, purchase what they need, then move on and forget about you. The customers you *do* get, then, you need to keep.

We think of this as "retention and return." *Retention* refers to keeping people who have already bought, and *return* refers to getting people back to your business. You want people who have bought from you to buy again, obviously, but you also want visitors who haven't purchased anything yet to keep coming back until they buy something. It typically takes a minimum of four touch points before someone is willing to buy from you. Fortunately, we can use systems and software to automate a lot of this—and that's where the real magic happens. Getting people to come back—and stay—is an art form that, once perfected, can pay dividends for years to come. Let's get into it.

START WITH A LEAD MAGNET

A lead magnet is a free resource, discount code, or tool a visitor to your website can get once they share a piece of personal information (usually a phone number or email address) so that you can stay in touch with them. By providing a special offer in return for a customer's contact info, you can reach them long after they've left your website or store.

At Bumblebee Linens, we offer customers a chance to spin a wheel of fortune to win valuable prizes in our store. This allows a person to earn discounts anywhere from 5 to 20 percent along with free merchandise. Every entry on the wheel is a winner, and once you win, you have to text a special message on your phone to redeem the prize. That way, we gain both an email and a phone number so that we can contact the customer in the future in two different ways. Other effective lead magnets include quizzes, guides, mini courses, and other free content.

Eric Bandholz of Beardbrand, which sells beard care products, asks his customers to take a quiz to determine what type of beard they have. To receive the results, they have to enter in their email, which allows Beardbrand to collect a ton of data from their customers so they can continue to market to the people who have already bought from them (and will likely buy again). In business, half the battle an entrepreneur fights is building an audience of potential customers and repeatedly exposing them to their brand. Once we have their contact information, that's when we can take them on a journey that keeps them in our world for as long as we can serve them.

AUTOMATING YOUR MARKETING

For our business, we try to automate and systematize as much as possible, using an email marketing service that immediately places the customer in one of a series of message sequences. I'll list them below, one at a time, so that you can see how we do this. All of the sequences described below are automatic. They are sent out to customers by a computer with no human intervention whatsoever. It took a little time to build all these, but now that this system exists, the whole thing runs like clockwork.

Pre-Purchase Sequence

As I mentioned, only 2 percent of customers will buy on their first visit. You have to contact your customer regularly so that when they are ready to buy, they think about your store and purchase whatever product or service you are offering at the time. You can't assume they know what you do or that they'll remember you weeks or months from now. You have to stay top of mind without being annoying. We do this through smart automations that keep us in touch with our customers without having to think about it ever. Our pre-purchase sequence is a series of emails sent roughly three days apart that is designed to introduce our brand to "cold" customers (people who have never made a purchase) and emphasize our unique value propositions. Here's a hypothetical five-email sequence we use that you can copy and apply to your own business.

1. Email #1: Welcome and thank them for joining your list. Provide the lead magnet you promised at sign-up.
2. Email #2: Share your brand story and unique value proposition. Tell the potential customer why they should buy from you.
3. Email #3: Provide product recommendations and steer the customer toward your best-selling products and services. Explain the value you provide and tell them exactly what to buy, eliminating any potential ambiguity or confusion.
4. Email #4: Provide social proof in the form of customer reviews, press mentions, and endorsements. Once again, emphasize

popular products so that they know other people are buying from you and raving about it. This will make the lead feel more comfortable buying from you, therefore increasing their trust in you.

5. Email #5: Invite them to join your community. Encourage them to follow you on social media (so that they don't miss an announcement, giveaway, discount, or whatever you offer on these various channels), and tell them to participate in any communities you might have (Discord group, Facebook group, etc.).

Abandoned Cart Sequence

If a customer views a product and does not complete their purchase, they are automatically sent an email that reminds them to come back and finish the transaction. Customers often window shop and forget to complete their purchase. By reminding them what was in their shopping cart, you can recover up to 30 percent of your lost sales.

The message doesn't have to be complicated. In our business we say, "We noticed that you started the checkout process but didn't finish your purchase. Click here to finish your transaction." The email displays photos of the products in the customer's shopping cart and has a single button that takes them directly to checkout. You may have seen this in other ecommerce platforms you use as a customer. It's an effective way to remind people that at one point they were going to buy something and didn't.

Re-engagement Sequence

A customer who has purchased from you once is 65 percent more likely to buy from you again. But customers generally have short memories, and you have to remind them to come back. In our business, for customers who have purchased once but haven't purchased in thirty days, we offer a coupon code with a small discount to entice them to come back. The message is short and simple and is something along the lines of: "It's been a while since we've seen you, and we've added a ton of new products since you last visited. Here's a coupon. Come on back!" If they haven't bought in sixty days, we then give them a bigger coupon—not too much, just the right amount to get them to come back. If they haven't bought in ninety days, we offer an even bigger coupon. If they make a purchase, no further emails are sent, and we never give discounts that are larger than necessary. It's just a strategy to stay top of mind and re-engage with customers.

Post-Purchase Follow-up Sequence

This sequence is activated once a customer makes a purchase to entice them to leave reviews or to make a subsequent purchase. Whenever someone makes a purchase, you always want to follow up. These emails don't have to be complicated. You just need to remind your customers that you exist. We use our post-purchase email sequence to solicit product reviews, get testimonials, introduce customers to new products, and take surveys. We also use this sequence to cross-sell related items. For example, we sell matching cocktail, lunch, and dinner napkins in our store. If a customer purchases cocktail napkins only, we automatically send an email to sell them matching lunch and dinner napkins. This way, we maximize the revenue for every customer.

In addition to the automated flows described above, which are set it and forget it, you should also manually email your customers at least once per week. Don't be afraid to email your potential customers. After all, they voluntarily signed up to your list! What you'll find is that every email you send makes you money.

Most people think you can overdo it with email, but I disagree. If people signed up for your list, knowing that you were going to sell to them, then you have permission to sell, as long as the offer is relevant. During the winter holidays, there's a period when we email our customers every single day for two weeks. No one ever complains, and every single email makes us money. In my experience, most businesses don't email enough, because they are afraid people will unsubscribe. But you *want* people to unsubscribe. You don't want to pay an email marketing company to keep tire-kickers as subscribers. If they aren't going to buy from you, you shouldn't be spending money on them. Sell what you have as confidently and as hard as you want. The people who want it will buy it, and those who don't, will leave. There's nothing wrong with that.

AUTOMATING CUSTOMER SERVICE

Providing great customer service is also a way to keep your customers for the long haul. When you run a business, you can imagine how many questions a company has to field every day. People want to know if you carry this item or that or if you have it in a different color. They want to know when you'll be back in stock, where their order is, are you open on Christmas, and so on.

These messages can come through a variety of channels, including social media, text messages, email, even the good old-fashioned telephone. In our company, each employee in our company is responsible for replying to these inquiries, and in many companies, there is an entire support team dedicated to replying to these messages all day long. That's a lot of time and energy and, well, money. How well does it work? Most people have no idea. "It's just the cost of doing business" is what I often hear. I hate that. Not to mention, is any of it working? And how do you keep track of it all?

When you have all this correspondence coming from different sources, it's hard to keep track of it. At first, it was overwhelming to even try; we kept repeating ourselves and stepping on each other's toes, occasionally missing an issue. It was messy and frustrating, sometimes even embarrassing. Fortunately, thanks to the technology gods, we found a solution. These days, there's almost always a way to automate a task that a person could make a mistake on.

Ultimately, we found a service called Gorgias that pushed all our customer contact channels through a single platform, allowing one person to reply to those requests from a single interface. This cut back on checking a bunch of different websites, keeping track of who received a response and when, and updating our database to log the interaction. It automatically pulls order data from your platform into emails so that you don't have to type.

If someone wants to know their tracking number, Gorgias detects that and allows you to use a canned template. You don't have to type a thing. All our employees have accounts on this interface, so that whenever they reply the software logs who does it. There's no manual tracking required and no need for faulty human memory to recollect who said what and when.

This goes beyond customer service, though, and straight to sales and marketing. We can track every reply and action that follows, then connect that interaction to a customer ID, making it a bottom-line issue. If a team member replies to an inquiry and that leads to a sale, we can even assign a dollar amount to that interaction. With this tool, we can now quantify customer service, which is amazing. It's no longer subjective. We know how much money each interaction and each rep is making the company. That's not a thing many businesses can boast, but thanks to a little easy tech, we can. Of course, there are qualitative interactions you can't connect back to the bottom line, but it's cool when you can. Nothing feels better than knowing that something you're paying for is actually making you money.

One of the goals in our business is to minimize the number of calls we receive. Calls take time, and that's the only nonrenewable resource an entrepreneur has. Any time we spend answering the same questions repeatedly could be applied to solving bigger problems. Our goal is to create a world-class customer experience where there is no need for call support. After all, who likes waiting on hold to speak to a customer service representative? Nobody.

Nonetheless, we still do get calls, and whenever we get a phone call, the most common question we receive is: "Where's my order, when will it be delivered, and what is the tracking information?" It's always the same problem, and it takes time and energy to respond each time, which means we've got an inefficiency.

Efficiency not only equals profit, it also means more free time for business owners to do more of what they love. Making things more efficient means you are also able to offer the best prices at the greatest value. Your customers get a better deal, better service—*all* of it. When we fix customer service issues, we free up time and money, and that's better for the business and the customers we serve.

Which is why we deployed robots, also known as chatbots, to talk to people with questions.

You saw that coming, right? Here's how it works. When you go on the Bumblebee Linens site now, there's a live chat window that opens up and one of the buttons says, "Where's my order?" When someone clicks that button, it automatically detects their email address if they're already logged into Facebook. Or they can enter their own email address if they're not. Once they do that, our website is pinged, and it tells them exactly where the order is. The same goes for when it will be delivered. They click the appropriate button, then they're taken to another page where they can calculate the delivery time and—voila!—question answered.

A simple automation that costs us less than $50 a month has cut down dramatically on the number of daily phone calls we receive, saving us dozens of hours every month. All of this is done automatically via a computer that sends pre-recorded, automated messages that pull live data from our system. There's very little tweaking or management involved. You just set it and forget it. Chatbot equals brilliance.

In my experience, it's not true that customers want personal attention. They just want quick and helpful service. The problem is that when they are speaking to a computer or a customer representative who hasn't been sufficiently trained or programmed to help the customer, then the result is frustration. These are just bad systems in action. The best way for you to keep a customer and have them coming back for more is to make your systems as efficient as possible. Automate as much as you possibly can, so that the margin of error is lower than it would be if a bunch of humans were messing with the customer's experience. All you need to succeed in business is to make useful things for people, deliver them to the customer on time and with excellence, and stay in regular communication with them. You'd be surprised how little of this you actually need to do. If a robot or computer can do a better job, why not let them? Save the brain power you have for solving other problems—like how to design your business in a way that will make you the happiest.

CHAPTER 11

Growth Is Expensive

Almost every entrepreneur aspires to grow their business. I've never met a business owner who didn't start out with a vision of building something bigger than how things began. This hunger for more is a typical trait of just about every business owner, and I'm no different. I never wanted to stay in that start-up phase of packing boxes every day and lugging them to the post office. But I learned the hard way that there is a significant cost to growth.

The entrepreneurial ambition to create something that's never been and take it as far as it can go can be a gift, but it can also be a curse. Nothing is more expensive than growing your business the wrong way. When you want to grow without any direction or constraint, you can easily destroy the very thing you're trying to build. My wife and I almost lost everything when my ambition got the better of me and we started scaling in ways that were unsustainable. In fact, Jen ended up losing her favorite hobby in the process, because we took her passion of embroidering and tried to milk it for everything it was worth. I'm grateful that we found a way out, but it wasn't easy.

Chalene Johnson, a serial entrepreneur and online influencer, has a similar story. Having started many businesses since the age of fifteen, Chalene has seen huge successes with the likes of Beachbody and TV infomercials, as well as more niche hits (that were far more profitable) in the world of Internet marketing and social media. But before all that, there was a messy middle.

Chalene struggled to balance business growth with her own ideals of what it meant to be a good mom, keep a clean house, and have a happy marriage. She did her best to make it to all her kids' activities, but because there was always something to be done in the business, it was hard to give her full attention to any single activity. "I was always there," she told me, "but I wasn't always present."

Early on in their shared entrepreneurial journey, Chalene and her husband, Bret, realized that if they didn't change the way they were doing things, they'd be playing "catch-up" their whole lives, chasing one opportunity after the next, never creating the life they truly wanted. Their businesses were making money, but the couple was mysteriously falling deeper and deeper into debt.

Financially, Chalene felt the pressure to work more, hustle harder, and turn things around. But with mounting piles of unfolded laundry and a never-ending list of tasks that weren't getting done, she began to feel like a failure as a mother, wife, and entrepreneur. This is common for most entrepreneurs: to succeed at work at the detriment of every other area in life.

While Chalene and Bret were building their business together, they were at the same time growing apart. Unbeknownst to her, their money problems were the consequence of Bret's gambling addiction. The couple agreed to go to therapy in an effort to repair their marriage and unravel the addiction. It was in therapy that Chalene realized that she, too, had an addiction. She was addicted to the hustle.

"There's a stigma associated with certain addictions," she told me, "like gambling or porn or drugs. But the same reasons why someone becomes addicted to any of those things is the same reason why people become addicted to work." And no matter what the addiction is, they can have the same devastating effects on your family, relationships, and mental health. Chalene was quick to blame her husband and send him to therapy, thinking she was fine. She had long believed that "work-a-holic" was a compliment, which she wore as a badge of honor. Until then, she had believed that to be successful, you needed to be addicted to work on some level. She soon learned how wrong she had been.

It took some time and intentional work for Chalene and Bret to build a better life, but they did it by creating rules and constraints that allowed them to manage their life and work as their businesses grew. And they were able to do it all without sacrificing everything they cared about for the next opportunity or dollar. I'll share more about how they did this later, but for now, just know that growth is overrated and almost every entrepreneur starts out with a sense of scarcity around opportunity.

We are all scared that this is the only time to succeed, that this is the only shot we'll ever get, and so we give up practically everything each time a temptation comes along. If you want to do this for the long haul, though, and you want your family and friends to know you, you're going to have to count the cost of what it takes to grow a business. There is, after all, a right and wrong way to do this—at least for the family-first entrepreneur.

WHAT IT TAKES TO GROW

These days, there are lots of low-risk ways to start a family-first business, but when we began, the simplest option for us was to sell a physical product online. We didn't want to get into brick-and-mortar or anything that would take us away from our kids and time together. Our goal was a simple business that we could automate as much as possible. Back then, there were people selling digital goods, but that was not as popular then as it is today. We didn't really know what we were getting ourselves into, but we thought we were playing it fairly conservatively. Little did we know how complicated it was about to get.

One of the main differences between ecommerce and, say, a digital store is that you actually have to buy inventory. This was brand new to us and involved way more risk than even I understood. In the beginning when you start your store, you may think, "If I can just make X, I'll replace my salary." That's largely how we thought of it, too: *If we can just make an extra $100K, we'll replace Jen's salary, and she can stay home with the kids.* It was a little more complicated than that, and that is the understatement of the decade.

Let's break this down here, just so we're clear on how most ecommerce businesses work. The concept is simple enough: You buy a product for cheap, and you sell it for more. That's basic business and how commerce has worked for centuries. If I can easily get something over here that is valuable to you, then trade it for something that is valuable to me, we have a deal. The trick is that what you are giving me must be worth more than what I got the thing for in the first place. Money is simply a symbol for the value we believe we are exchanging. So in everyday terms, this means if I can get a water bottle for $2 and sell it to you for $5, then that's good business. Maybe you could go find the water bottle for $2, but it would take a lot of your time and energy, and $3 is not that big of a deal for you, so you pay the extra money to save yourself time and energy, which you can then use to go do something that earns you more than $3. Overall, pretty simple, right?

Not exactly.

Most people don't realize that when you start buying and reselling goods at a larger scale, you have to start carrying inventory. As your sales spike, you have to buy more than you currently need. This can be good in some cases: You can buy a lot of goods up front and get a discount. If you order, for example, a thousand water bottles, you might be able to get them for $1 apiece instead of $2. That's a good deal, right? It is if you can sell all thousand water bottles.

But what if you can only sell five hundred? Or two hundred? There is a point at which it makes more sense to not carry so much inventory. But you also never want to go out of stock, because if you run out, your customer will go to a competitor, and you may lose their business forever.

So you start your business, begin selling water bottles, and soon the sales increase. You get nervous and want to keep up with demand, so you buy more inventory. The supplier sees the increased order and calls you, offering a special discount if you order a lot more, but you have to pay for it up front. Not to mention, if you don't sell it all, you have to pay storage costs. So you start selling to get rid of your inventory. Then, you order more. Maybe you don't have enough cash to make these large, up-front inventory orders, so you put it all on a credit card, which makes you nervous, so you sell even harder and more frantically. Soon, you've lost track of what's what and you're using today's sales to pay for yesterday's expenses. It becomes unwieldy to keep track of, especially if it happens quickly. You have no idea if you're making a profit or not, and this describes most people selling physical products.

As you become more successful, you end up floating a lot more money. A lot of money comes in, a lot of money goes out. How profitable are you, exactly? It's hard to say, and let's be honest: You didn't pay much attention in that one accounting class you took in college. Or maybe your CPA or part-time bookkeeper isn't experienced enough to manage cashflow at this level. Let's say you've got a million dollars coming in through the store each year, but you are also carrying half a million in inventory. Maybe even a million, because you really wanted to stock up and not run out. This is money you had to pay up front, as you know, and what happens if the sales suddenly slow down? What if you have to liquidate your inventory, because you have other expenses and can't afford to pay people to manage this robust and complicated system that you didn't understand while you were building it? What do you do in the case of a recession when suddenly water bottles are no longer necessary? This can all start to feel pretty stressful.

This may sound unique to ecommerce, and in some ways, it is, but it actually applies to all businesses where you have to invest a lot of cash up front, float your own money before you even get any returns, and hope for the best. Most physical-goods companies work this way, and many service-based businesses do as well. Almost all tech start-ups do, and any digital-goods businesses that start scaling eventually require an investment of capital either into creating more digital goods or hiring a team. Regardless of the type of business you have, you get the idea of how quickly things can get out of hand, and how hard they are to manage once they do.

Success is not always what it seems to be. It can be quite the burden and, in its own way, a unique problem. As the stress builds and worst-case scenarios keep you up at night, you inevitably start looking at your competitors. You are trying to stay on top of it all, and growth seems to be the only way out. You notice that your competitors are using *this* tool, so, you think to yourself, you had better install it and start using it. You see your friends joining new mastermind groups, and these guys seem to be killing it (at least, from what you can tell watching their highlight reels on social media), so you do the same.

You know for a fact that your good buddy in this one group made a million dollars in their last launch. "I didn't make a million dollars in my last launch," you say to yourself, "so I better set my bar a lot higher. After all, I don't belong in this mastermind group unless I can achieve similar results . . ." Right? Of course, you never bothered to ask your friend what it cost to make that million dollars. But who cares? It's a million dollars. You'd have to be a real dummy to not make a profit off that. So, without really thinking too much about it, you emulate your friends and peers, copying what you see them doing on the outside without really understanding how it works or feels on the inside.

This is how most businesses die. Not from selling too little. But from selling too quickly. Growing too fast. If you are lucky enough to get your business off the ground—and that part is legitimately hard—the next greatest risk of failure is your own ego. Your own greed. Look, I'm not going to tell you to be humble or not want to do big, bold things. Go for it. I'll cheer you on all the way. But be careful how quickly you do this and how you do it. Because if you don't pay close attention, you could easily grow this thing right into the ground.

In our own story, as Jen and I came closer to hitting a million dollars in annual revenue, I started to lose sight of what we were doing and why.

I don't know what it is about zeroes, but adding an extra one at the end of our "annual sales" statement was more than a little enticing. As we got closer to a million bucks, I told my wife with absolute conviction, "I want to have a seven-figure business."

One year, we were close to hitting that landmark. As we got closer to the end of the year, we didn't think we were going to make it based on our current trajectory, so I said, "Okay, let's increase our ad spend. Let's start blasting the heck out of my list. Even though the ads are barely profitable, let's just do it. Let's achieve this seven-figure goal." I know for a fact I'm not the only guy who's ever done this. Most of my friends who have come close to such a goal have done the same. It's exciting! You get to say, "I made a million dollars this year!" Even if only on paper. But pretty soon, you're stressing about a goal that has no bearing on your happiness whatsoever. In fact, it is often more costly than growing slowly and maintaining solid margins. But here you are now, working toward an arbitrary goal that gives you something to talk about at your next mastermind meeting.

The year we tried to hit a million dollars for the first time, we were behind in production and short-staffed. We didn't actually have the staff to fulfill the large volume orders necessary to hit that goal, and I didn't care. I blasted my email list constantly and burned out a lot of trusting subscribers. I increased the ad spend at the expense of profitability (against my better judgment) and ended up working sixty- to seventy-hour weeks during the holiday season with my wife. It sucked. This was a far cry from the freedom and quality-of-life goals we had set at the very beginning. But we made it. We hit our goal by burning out our list, exhausting ourselves, and killing our profit margins. It felt good . . . for about a day.

And then, you know what? I felt like we had to do it again. This was now the new bar, and the following year, we had to do more. We had to go bigger. We were now on a hamster wheel that we didn't know how to slow down or get off of. This went on for years: me working like a dog, my wife being dragged along on the process, and both of us doing stuff we didn't want to do to hit some arbitrary goal. We sacrificed a lot of financial and personal margin—and for what? Mainly because my peers around me were "killing it." Or so I thought.

THE TRUTH ABOUT SCALING

Entrepreneurs can set arbitrary and aggressive goals that end up causing a loss of focus on what really matters. Once I burnt out from this experience, I started to get real with myself and some of my peers. I began to dig deep into the finances of my business and ask more pointed questions of my friends. Did you really make a million dollars, I wondered? How did that work, exactly?

I was surprised to hear how often the numbers were inflated. "Well," they might say, "that's what the launch did, but most of those are payment plans for the next twelve months. We sold just under a million dollar's worth of products but only brought in about $380K in cash."

One guy I knew grew his online course business from about half a million dollars to over a million in annual revenue. It was an aggressive growth trajectory, but he really wanted to get that extra zero, and I understand why. When he looked at the numbers, though, he was surprised to see that the year he made a million dollars in sales, he spent $910,000 to do so. It was the most stressful year of his life, he said. Call me crazy, but there are probably easier ways to bring home $90,000.

Part of the family-first approach to entrepreneurship, which I admit I learned through a lot of failure, is knowing what is enough and intentionally choosing to reject the hustle mentality when you've hit your limit. More is not always better. In fact, sometimes, more does not even mean more. When you make more money, you often have to spend more, and sometimes that means lower profit margins and more work. Who wants that? Sometimes I hear entrepreneurs talk about impact, but more often than not, that seems to simply be another word for ego.

These days, I don't care about "scaling" or growing just to grow. I want a business with healthy margins that only requires a handful of hours a week for me to run. I want to be able to eat dinner with my family each night and go to bed at a decent hour. I want to be able to spend quality time with my wife and go on date nights each week. I want to be able to take care of myself and never miss a major moment in my kids' lives. Because I ditched the daily grind of trying to hit pointless goals and stopped hustling to impress my friends, I am able to do just that.

More small business owners are waking up to the reality of what they really want. Most entrepreneurs don't want to be Steve Jobs or Jeff Bezos—not really. They don't want to sacrifice everything for the sake of "changing the world." I don't. What they really want—what I believe is motivating most of us who are in this game—is not to scale into infinity. It's freedom, both in terms of time and money. If I can work fewer hours, have greater flexibility in my schedule, and make more money than if I were at a day job, isn't that better than killing myself to build something that I might be able to sell someday?

Most people who believe the hustle myth are deluding themselves into thinking that if they work like a dog every day for years on end, they'll get the freedom they hope for . . . some day. But most burn out, crash and burn, or simply get to a finish line that they don't know how to enjoy. The truth is that you can have all the freedom you want now—without sacrificing what matters most to you. It takes a little courage to do this, a willingness to follow the road less traveled, but it's worth it. And like I said, more and more people are realizing this for themselves and creating the kind of companies and lifestyles they used to dream of.

Remember Chalene Johnson, whom I mentioned earlier in this chapter? When she and her husband, Bret, hit a wall in their personal life while growing a business that demanded more of their time and energy every day, they had to step back and create what they called a "Priority Clarity Statement." This is a detailed and specific set of rules and guidelines that they revisit in each season of life to help them make everyday decisions regarding their businesses, personal lives, and family.

On this list were rules like when they'd be done working every day and how often each of them could travel for work every month. They also made a commitment to never miss a kid activity where they both weren't present (barring an occasional monthly trip where only one of the parents would attend the activity). These guidelines brought tremendous clarity to their life and work, but it also produced initial conflict.

Of course, they weren't perfect at reinforcing these boundaries once they were set, but Bret and Chalene were careful to talk in code around their kids when one of them got off-track. They used their Priority Clarity Statement as a rubric for making decisions and evaluating opportunities. It was a guide. One of the key questions they'd ask when a new business idea or growth opportunity arrived was "Is this going to be helpful or hurtful to the emotional health and stability of our family?"

Soon after establishing their priorities in writing, Chalene had an opportunity to appear on television that she was excited about. However, she realized it was going to take her away from her family and contradict this essential value she and Bret had established. They would have made a lot of money, but it wouldn't have helped them create the life that they wanted. So they said no.

According to Chalene, these decisions are easier to make once you've written them down. "It's so easy to talk yourself into something that you have the sneaking suspicion is not in the best interests of your relationships," she said. Putting it on paper makes it something more concrete, harder to break. You've made a commitment to not only what's important to you but how you are willing to grow.

When you're starting out, you think your current opportunity is the only one that will ever come along. But after many decades of building many businesses, Chalene and her husband of twenty-eight years can attest there's always another opportunity around the corner. But you only get so many years with your kids living under your roof, and you only get so many evenings or anniversaries with your spouse. Don't sacrifice those precious gifts for the next "big break." These chances are not as rare as you might think.

AMANDA AUSTIN'S LITTLE SHOP OF MINIATURES

Amanda Austin runs a six-figure business selling dollhouse furniture over at ShopofMiniatures.com. She usually works between ten and twenty hours a week. But lately, she is barely working at all because she has a seven-week-old (at the time of this writing). It took her roughly three years to get to this point, but she did it.

Amanda's Little Shop of Miniatures specializes in dollhouse miniatures and dollhouse kits. She has two suppliers, one for kits and one for dollhouse miniatures, but the majority of her sales come from the miniatures. In her store, she has everything you can imagine: a dollhouse sofa, dollhouse food, actual dolls, and all kinds of other random items. She even has miniature electric chairs! It's a much more popular hobby than many realize (certainly more than I did!). Most people who shop at her store are hobbyists, primarily older women, although there are men as well. The men tend to buy more dollhouse-building supplies, so she's added baseboards and electric kits to her store.

She chose this niche of dollhouses while doing keyword research. It kept coming up as a competitive keyword compared to her spreadsheet of other business ideas that she was entertaining. When she looked at her competitor's sites, they weren't done very well, and she saw an opportunity to do it better. As a kid, Amanda's grandmother had a dollhouse, and she spent all her money going to a dollhouse furniture store at the local mall. Eventually, the store closed, but she still had the dollhouse full of miniatures. She had an affinity for the niche, but it wasn't the only thing she was interested in. She had passion for the product, but there was a lot that she had to learn on the business side of things.

Amanda is a one-woman show. She does the customer service, fulfillment, and everything in between. The business is all drop-ship, which means she doesn't have to deal with any fulfillment or warehousing issues. It's all handled by a third party. Her supplier has a warehouse not too far from her house—about a two-hour drive—and she has been able to visit several times. She views the workers there as part of her team even though they aren't technically her employees. There are over three thousand items in her store, and she could easily add another ten thousand if she wanted.

Like many entrepreneurs, Amanda's goal in starting her store was all about personal freedom. She had been in corporate America for fifteen years and always felt like a fish out of water. As a talented and hardworking person, she got promoted regularly, which kept her stuck in the employee hamster wheel of success. In her last five years, she worked in insurance and had all of the top designations. Even with these achievements, though, she just never liked any of her jobs. She didn't enjoy taking orders and never understood why she had to work an eight-hour day if she could get the same amount of work done in four hours. Amanda realized that she would never be happy long term working in a corporate environment; it just wasn't for her. And if she simply switched jobs, the same problems would be somewhere else. She realized all of this before having children.

Then, right before she got married, Amanda started laying the groundwork for the life she really wanted. She didn't want to have to work a set number of hours. She didn't want to have to go to work at all anymore. Her biggest hurdle was her own self-doubt. Could she really create the kind of life she wanted, working a fraction of the time she was used to while still making a similar amount of money? Then she became a mom, and her priorities shifted even more toward family.

After having kids, Amanda knew there was no way she wanted to work a forty-hour week ever again. And what *for*? What we consider a traditional workweek was invented by a society that needed people to spend a minimum of eight hours a day in a factory, standing at an assembly line assembling widgets just to meet the company quota . . . Right? What use, then, is such a convention for a knowledge worker today? It all felt pretty outdated. Amanda wanted to be present for her kids and be as hands-on a mother as possible. Her goal wasn't to make a ton of money; she just wanted to replace her corporate income or come close to it without having to incur the cost of childcare. She didn't set out on her entrepreneurial journey with a specific vision for the future other than that. Just the freedom to be a good mom—that's all she wanted.

Sometimes, Amanda thinks about having her own warehouse and employees, but right now she's chosen to limit the growth of her company, because it's just not the right time in her life to do that. This is an important discipline for many family-first entrepreneurs: it's not that they are opposed to growth, just that they understand everything comes with a cost. As the saying goes, you can have anything you want; you just can't have everything, at least not all at once. Getting clear on this is what we all need to do. You don't want to chase a certain kind of "growth" only to discover that you've sacrificed the one thing you really want. Right now, Amanda is only spending about five hours a week on the store and the rest is spent with her family. She makes the equivalent of a competitive, full-time corporate salary (over $100,000 a year). On an ideal day, she'll spend her kid's nap time in the store doing things like writing a blog post, adding new products, reconciling QuickBooks, and answering customer questions.

The hardest part of becoming an entrepreneur for Amanda was believing it was possible. She had a "good job" with great benefits and job security. Many of her peers thought she was nuts to leave all that to sell dollhouses. Now, if her store doesn't continue to grow at all and stays where it is, that would be a great income and a really good life. She gets to essentially be a full-time mom and part-time entrepreneur with all the money and freedom she could ever want.

WHAT MAKES YOU HAPPY?

How do you, as an ambitious entrepreneur, not grow in the wrong direction or in the wrong way? How do you not fall into the typical trap of hustling and grinding only to wake up later, realizing you spent your energy in the wrong place? Oftentimes, it's really about figuring out what makes you happy. This sounds like a cliché, but it's true. What held Amanda back was what other people thought. What nearly drove my marriage and business into the ground was what my friends were doing. In the end, though, none of that matters. No one can tell you what makes you happy, and it's a little different for everyone.

For me, at least, it's not just one thing. In fact, there are four aspects to my happiness, and they all work together to create a meaningful and fulfilled life. In my case, the four areas of fulfillment are: wealth, mental stimulation, family, and social interaction. Let's break each of those down, because they represent areas of human need that are applicable to most, if not all, of humanity. To be happy, what you need to do is take a look at your life and figure out what are the minimum thresholds for each category. Let's take them one at a time.

Wealth

Most people start businesses to make money. It's not just about the cause or passion or purpose behind it. Everyone needs money to live, right? So it's pretty simple: How much money do you spend in a given year? What are your goals in life? What do you want, and what does it cost? By no means am I arguing that you go be a monk. Just figure out what you really want and create a lifestyle that allows you to get it. If you can do all that in a corporate job, by all means do it. But if the place you're in right now isn't offering you fulfillment in each area of your life that is important to you, then it's time to change some things. And starting a business—when you do it the right way—is one of the best ways to help you create the life you want.

Some people want more extravagant things than others, and that's fine. You get to decide what matters to you, but be sure to ask yourself why you want the things you want. Most people, if you ask them directly and sincerely, will say what they really want is to spend more time with the people they love, doing the things they want to do. I've never heard someone say in response to the question "What makes you happy?" that they really just want to go into an office for forty hours a week for the rest of their lives. That's telling. Most of us, when it really comes down to our top priorities, want to feel free to do the things we want. And so what is the cost of that freedom? How much money do you need to live the life you want?

Most people aren't going to be spending millions of dollars on themselves. I have one friend who is an entrepreneur and lives really well. He spends $150,000 per year just on himself, and it's an extravagant lifestyle. Trust me. You don't need as much as you think, and it won't cost nearly what you imagine. All you need to do is figure out what your expenses are, what you ultimately need to be happy, and maybe a handful of fun experiences or things that would be nice to have.

We spend about $150,000 a year for our family of four, and we live pretty well. This isn't that much money when you start thinking like an entrepreneur. Can we find a way to create enough value that we're able to bring home at least that much money to support our lifestyle? Of course, we can and we do. We bring in a lot more than that, which allows us to save, invest, and purchase other bonuses on occasion. We don't need those extravagances, but it's nice to be able to buy them when we can. That's just us, though. What you need is up to you.

You need to figure out what you want to satisfy your wealth needs. Oftentimes, it's not as much as you think you need, so just get clear on whatever that number is. I can tell you from experience that few entrepreneurs do this, and they'd save themselves a lot of hassles if they started here. All things considered, it's not that hard to make that much money selling a simple product to a specific niche. So if your business is already generating twice what your minimum wealth number is, that's good enough, right? That way, you spend half, get to keep half, and you're good. That's super simple math, and we haven't taken into account things like expenses and taxes and whatnot, but you get the idea.

Your best life is not as complicated as you might think it is. Figure out how much money you need to bring home to be good, and find a way to do it. "More" is not a number. You need something specific to aim for, so that when you hit it, you know. You don't have to keep pushing to add another zero; you can know when you're good on the wealth side, so that you can focus on other areas of your life. After all, everybody knows money doesn't make you happy by itself.

Mental Stimulation

The second aspect of creating happiness, for me, is mental stimulation. This is different, of course, for different people, but most people need some kind of intellectual challenge to feel like they're growing as a human. I know for myself that my mind requires near-constant stimulation. I could never just retire and live on the beach for the rest of my life. I always need to be learning, growing, and acquiring new skills. I've met many entrepreneurs who had fantastic exits from their companies and thought they "made it" only to discover that selling their company wasn't the finish line they thought. After a few months of traveling, they'd admit to me, "I'm SO bored. I'm gonna start another business." That's pretty typical, especially for those of us who like building things. We don't want to be done; we want to be doing things. And the game of business is not about finishing; it's about always having something new to start. Again, I'm not anti-growth; we just want to be growing the right things at the right time, and your mind should be one of those things.

Certainly, one area of mental stimulation can be your own company, but you have to figure out whether your business is already stimulating you enough without overdoing it. Oftentimes with the business, once you have a certain formula for success down, it can become a little monotonous. Most businesses, once you've optimized them, start to become necessarily boring. In the case of ecommerce, most of the work is just filling orders, day in and day out. Once you're making money, having established a solid system that allows the business to run like clockwork, you'll probably get a little bored. That's normal. Be careful here, as a lot of entrepreneurs see this as a sign they need to change something. Not necessarily. Don't burn something down that's working just because you've reached stability. This is why you want to figure out the minimum amount that will keep you stimulated.

What I do with my businesses every year is I try to tackle one new marketing aspect. One year was Facebook Messenger. I spent the entire year figuring out how to create Facebook Messenger chat bots. A couple years ago, it was SMS. A few years before that, it was Facebook ads, and before that it was Google ads. Another was podcasting. Recently, it was YouTube, then TikTok.

I just pick one thing each year that poses some sort of intellectual challenge for me, and I spend the year figuring it out and then applying it to the business. It's a simple way to learn a new skill, serve my need for mental stimulation, and since I can usually connect it to the bottom line in some way, it doesn't fall by the wayside. I'm learning, having fun acquiring a new skill, but I'm also working. So I don't ever have to decide between making money and my own growth.

I know this is a problem for many entrepreneurs, but I don't have shiny object syndrome. I don't try to do too many things at once. I just do one thing a year, and getting good at that one thing is usually enough to keep me stimulated. What I've found is that many people who can't concentrate on a single goal have never tried it. They're afraid of picking the wrong thing or risking it all on one idea that may not work.

What I've learned is that when you really figure out what makes you happy, the simplest things can keep you occupied. You don't have to do it all once you know the few things you really need to live a good life. Something I really liked about my day job was that I was always working with brilliant people from MIT, Stanford, Cal, Princeton, Yale, etc. Sometimes, with your business, working with smart people is enough to stay stimulated. You have to figure it out for yourself, though. If your business is already making enough money, maybe you can have a side hobby that occupies your mind. Don't neglect this aspect of your growth, though. It'll make every other area better. If you keep learning new things, don't you think that'll affect how much money you're able to make? Of course it will.

Family

The next thing you want to figure out is your loved ones. This includes both family and friends. You always have to remember why you started your job in the first place, whatever it is. Most people want freedom that they don't have. And what do you do with that freedom? Well, you spend it with the people you care about, right? And so you have to get clear on who exactly it is that you care most about.

How does this work practically? It's easy. Figure out what your perfect day is. Imagine it right now, in your mind's eye. Not every single day can obviously be a perfect day, but if you have a sense of the ideal, you have a clear target. If I have one or two good days out of the week where I get to do whatever I want, which includes spending time with my loved ones, then that usually is good enough for me. I find this incredibly fulfilling, as simple as it sounds, and the fact that I have a perfect day in mind makes it possible.

My perfect day consists of working a little bit in the morning, playing a little bit of tennis or lifting weights in the afternoon, having lunch with my wife and dinner with the whole family, then hanging out with my kids in the evening. It's a pretty simple day, and it's wonderful. As long as I have a couple of those days per week, I'm great. I remember when that felt like a fight to accomplish, and now it feels entirely natural.

Decide how much time you need with your family and what's going to make you happy. Your perfect day doesn't have to look like mine, but as is the case with money, you may be surprised by how little you need and how simple it can be.

Human beings are not complicated creatures, in fact. What we need is quite simple. We need shelter, food, a sense of belonging, and mental well-being. Everything else is just nice to have. Personally, I make an effort to attend every single one of my kids' sporting events. That's one of my priorities, and it may not be for everyone, but I found I didn't like myself when I was missing significant experiences in my kids' lives and then making excuses for it. Being that guy didn't make me happy, so I changed it.

Social Interaction

Sometimes, family is not enough. I love my wife and kids. I love working for myself and experiencing the mental stimulation involved in tackling a difficult problem. But I also need to be stimulated socially, to be around other people who challenge me and bring out the best in me, even if that simply means making me laugh.

As human beings, we all need community, and that extends beyond our immediate families. Our species has been organizing itself into tribal units for millennia, and this is not a need that has gone away in the twenty-first century. In spite of the opportunities to connect with people all over the world via technology, we all need a night out with friends once in a while. Significant time with like-minded peers can feed your soul.

Sometimes, if you've been dealing with kids all day, you just want to hang out with some other adults. Sometimes you need a night away from your spouse. This is normal and necessary, yet many entrepreneurs get so lost in growing their business that they forget to regularly connect with others. If your business is taking you away from basic social interactions, that's not good and your work will ultimately suffer. You need to find the time to get away for a night and recharge; this is more important than most people realize and, therefore, easy to neglect.

Personally, I only really need to see my friends every other week or so. Once or twice a month is more than enough for me to feel stimulated socially; and yet, if I don't plan it, I can easily drift into seasons in which I go months without seeing "the guys." I need interaction with people who make me take things less seriously, as well as those who are smart and driven. As long as I get that every now and then, I'm good. I also have to make this time a priority, or it doesn't happen.

Figure out what this means for you and allocate the time to make it a priority. Figure out what the minimum thresholds are for what you need for each category in life, then prioritize hitting those. Anything over those minimums is great; you can consider that gravy. Just don't kill yourself to go after something you've already achieved. When you know you've already won the lottery, you can relax. You don't have to grow anymore. You can sit back and enjoy the life you've created. If you want to keep going after that, you can do it with ease and enjoyment.

CHAPTER 12

Prioritize Profit, Not Sales

Entrepreneurs deal with all kinds of challenges, one of which is the pressure to continually grow at all costs, so they can gain bragging rights about revenue. But having done that and burnt out my whole team and exhausted most of our resources, I can tell you that it isn't really worth it. Business is not about the top-line sales numbers—at least, not the kind of business we're talking about building in this book. It's about selling a quality product to people who want it, and doing it in a way where everybody wins in the long run. This means you have to keep some of the money you make and don't blow it all on company Maseratis.

The family-first entrepreneur knows that what really matters is creating the best profit margin possible so that you can enjoy time with your family and whatever freedoms are important to you. In order to do this, we've got to control our expenses, sell smartly, and optimize our businesses for what matters most.

But what *is* profit, exactly?

Pardon the high school economics lesson, but profit is what's left over after you've paid all your bills. You sell the product to the customer, cover all your expenses including cost of goods sold and any overhead you might have (staff, software, office costs, etc.), pay Uncle Sam his due, then what's left is what you get to keep as the business owner. You can invest this extra into growing the business, hiring more staff members, or simply disbursing some or all of it to yourself to enjoy personally. That is your right as a business owner and a really fun part of playing this game. Surprisingly, though, few business owners seem to know or care about profit, and this baffles me.

Profit is the lifeblood of your business. Without it, you are confined to living month to month, paying off last month's expenses with this month's sales, always feeling like you're playing catch-up—because you are. This is the equivalent of living paycheck to paycheck, a stressful reality for many people, business owners included. I'm willing to bet, though, that this is not why you became an entrepreneur, to wonder where your next pay day is going to come from and hoping for the best.

To live a truly free life, you can't be worried about how you're going to cover next month's expenses. You've got to get ahead of the feed-the-monster routine that so many business owners find themselves in. But how? Well, first we've got to define what we mean by *profit*. Making a profit in business, by the way, is not something that just happens. It's a discipline that is developed over time and reinforced constantly. As author Mike Michalowicz shares in his groundbreaking book *Profit First*, "Profit is not an event. It's a habit." Failure to recognize the necessity of this will likely result in a short lifespan for your business. You've got to watch your numbers and educate yourself on the financial well-being of your company. This is no one's job but yours. Even if you end up hiring a CFO at some point, you as the owner still need to know what your numbers are. And unless this comes naturally to you, it may take time and focus. Trust me: It'll be worth it.

This means you've got to start and grow your business with a keen eye on what matters most, which is what's left over when you're done paying the piper. In fact, you want to begin with how much you want to make first and budget your expenses accordingly. By prioritizing profit, spending your money smartly to ensure you maintain your margins, you ensure that you actually have money left over. Focusing on maximizing profit gives you the lifestyle you hoped for without having to give up too much to get there.

THERE'S NOTHING WRONG WITH BEING FRUGAL

Maybe this is a cultural thing because I'm Asian, but I'm cheap. I'll own it. I hate paying for things that I don't need, and I can find a reason to not pay for lots of things. One of the temptations facing many entrepreneurs is the decision to throw money at things that don't actually generate a return on investment. Like the latest tools and gadgets, for example. Starting a business is expensive, and once you figure out exactly what you need, you still have to watch where your money is going, or before you know it, you'll be out of cash. It's easy to think you're doing great only to get hit with a huge tax bill you weren't expecting and wonder where all the money went.

It's common to see people quit their jobs and go into business for themselves only to spend way too much trying to look good to their competitors, peers, and customers until they realize they aren't making real money. This is a pitfall for a lot of early entrepreneurs, especially when the cash starts pouring in.

If you've never made $50,000 in a month and suddenly you experience an explosion in sales, it's tempting to think of that cash as "your" money, but it's not. That money belongs to the business; in fact, a good chunk of it, depending on where in the world you live, belongs to the government. Some of it even belongs to the customer because you have to use those resources to ensure the end user gets what they paid for. It's not even fifty grand you're looking at. At best, it may be only thirty; or if you're like a lot of business owners, the number may be closer to zero.

Many businesses are operating at a deficit, spending more than they're making, slowly edging toward bankruptcy. But this shouldn't surprise us. How many people do you know who live above their means? They spend more than they make, getting by on credit cards and lines of credit and who knows what else. If they're lucky, they have just enough savings to make it through another year and maybe a little retirement tucked away. If something devastating were to happen to them or their business, they'd be in serious trouble. This is how many, if not most, people live. These same people who do not manage their personal finances repeat the same habit when they build a business.

All that to say: There's nothing wrong with being frugal.

As already stated, I don't spend money on anything I don't necessarily need. I loathe paying for any kind of recurring expenses, even if it's only a few dollars a month. In the world of ecommerce, it's easy to get nickel-and-dimed on apps. They're only ten dollars a month and easy to add, so someone who's just starting out may naively think they need to get all these tools to run their business. Whenever I see one of these nonessential tools taking advantage of some poor, unsuspecting beginner, it pisses me off—especially when I dissect the app and figure out what it actually does.

I don't pay for anything with recurring fees, if I can help it. Instead, what I'll do is write the app myself if I can do it in a week or less. Even if it only saves me ten dollars a month, it's a small personal victory. You might be thinking that's not the best use of my time, and that's fair. But the average Shopify user uses between seven and ten apps, most of which cost between twenty and fifty dollars per month. So we're talking about saving potentially up to five hundred dollars a month.

Now, imagine you use these apps for the next five years. That's $30,000 you just saved. Tell me, was it worth a few weeks of your time to find a way to avoid the monthly charge? For some people, the answer may be no, and that's totally fine. It's not for me to tell you how to spend your money. I enjoy building these things, so it's fun to find little ways to save money. I am also always thinking about the big picture; if I can spend a week writing a piece of code that saves me thousands of dollars in the long run, those are resources I can use elsewhere or money I don't have to make. Which allows our family to live simply, and I don't have to work more than necessary to provide for us.

So anything that carries recurring revenue, I try to create myself.

Granted, you may not be able to do the same, but the principle here is clear: You need to pay attention to the little ways in which cash flows out of your business. It all adds up, and if you can find ways to minimize that or even spend more in the short term and save in the long run, it may be worth it. I run a few online businesses and do all kinds of things my peers would never think to do.

For example, instead of paying hundreds of dollars per month for on-line video webinar services like WebinarJam, I just use YouTube. Instead of doing the same for online course platforms, I use free WordPress plugins to do the same. Now, there's nothing wrong with investing in good tools that help you serve your customers better or make more money, but often entrepreneurs assume these are necessary expenses when, in fact, they may not be.

My rule of thumb is nothing is necessary until you test it. See what you can get away with by trying to keep expenses at a minimum. Try it for ninety days, see how far you can get without spending money on something new. At worst, you'll find there are things you need to invest in that you can't live without. But at least you'll know. You won't have to assume or take someone else's word for it. And if you find yourself really needing something—a service, an extra set of hands, an app— see if there are any free or low-cost alternatives to the standard solution. The end result of such an experience is that you will likely increase your profit margin or at the very least know for sure what you need and what you don't.

For the family-first entrepreneur, profit means freedom. The fewer financial commitments you have, the more options are available to you. And the more options you have, the more free you will feel. When it comes to managing expenses, keep your eyes open and don't assume all expenses are necessary. Figure out what your cost centers are and fight to minimize those as much as possible. In the long run, it'll mean more options for you—and that's what this game is all about.

This goes back to self-sufficiency. I don't want to be beholden to anyone or anything to run my business, and every little service I pay ten or twenty dollars a month for is yet another way in which I am giving away my freedom. I didn't start my business to give other businesses money and access to my customer data and who knows what else. I did it so that I could live the kind of life I wanted and make good money doing so. If you have a business need for an app, for example, but can't write code to save your life, you can always hire someone on Fiverr or Upwork for a onetime fee, thus saving yourself the monthly expense.

Whenever you think about monthly expenses, don't just look at what it's going to cost you this month. Ask yourself, am I going to be happy in five years seeing this expense on my monthly list of bills? Or are you going to add up all these expenses and wonder what else you could have done with that money? Will it have been worth it to find a way to save that money so that you could be more in control of what you do? I also think of the time value of money. When you sell your business, every dollar saved is really four dollars. The reason for this is typically because the multiple to sell an ecommerce business is often four times earnings before interest, taxes, depreciation, and amortization (EBITDA). If you think of compounding interest, then, a dollar is really worth much more than a dollar twenty years down the line.

Doing things yourself not only saves you money but removes the risk of putting your trust in an outside person or service. I've been burned so many times with various software tools and companies failing me at the worst possible moment. Our old email marketing software banned us during the holiday season because of some weird flag that hit our account. This was our busiest time of year, and we couldn't afford to be in "email jail." We ended up getting blacklisted on this platform and never reinstated.

As far as I'm aware, we didn't do anything wrong except have a great business. This led to my wanting as much control over the business as possible. Many of my friends have experienced similar situations, seeing software tools they pay for suddenly locking their accounts or banning them for no reason. It's equally as dangerous to rely on third party marketplaces like Amazon or eBay to generate all of your revenue. John

Rampton was running a multi-million-dollar business selling storage containers and other organizational products through Amazon. At one point, one of his products had over 100,000 reviews. But when he wasn't able to fulfill his orders on time, Amazon temporarily shut him down. Eighteen hours later, they reinstated his seller accounts but shortly after that, they banned him again and refused to turn the account back on.

After multiple attempts at contacting everyone he knew at the company, John and his team decided to shut things down. In retrospect, if he had been selling on other sites instead of just Amazon, he would have been able to weather the storm. But not when he basically lost 90 percent of his revenue overnight. It's a big risk to put the fate of your company in someone else's hands—don't do it.

Oftentimes, the tools you use to run your business will for no apparent reason and without explanation hike their prices. I've seen companies double their rates overnight. Of course, we all depend on other people and services for help, but you want to be as self-reliant as possible. Isn't this what you signed up for: to be in control? Every dollar you spend on someone or something else outside of your company is a vote of confidence in someone else's abilities and integrity. Spend it carefully.

As an entrepreneur, your expenses are not out of your control. You have more say over what you pay than you may realize. Anything that you have control over, you have a say in. This is why I like building my own solutions, because it means I am not playing by someone else's rules. You and I most likely didn't get in this game of entrepreneurship to have anyone, especially not some mighty tech company, tell us what to do.

Watch your expenses. Limit them wherever possible. Cut anything you can, especially when it incurs a monthly payment. Employees, of course, are the worst example of this and one of the greatest cost centers (and you know how I feel about employees). Instead of hiring humans to answer emails and talk to customers, consider using email marketing solutions. Instead of having to correspond with your customers one-on-one, human-to-human, you could create a chat bot that answers your frequently asked questions. Computers are always cheaper than humans.

At the very least, find a way to batch these interactions. Inefficiencies are expensive and unnecessary. The more efficient you become, the more profitable you are, and the more profitable, the freer you become.

GET PAID WHAT YOU'RE WORTH

To make the most from your business, though, you can't just watch expenses; penny pinching will only get you so far, after all. To truly thrive as an entrepreneur, you also have to charge as much as you possibly can. You have to make every dollar go as far as it can, and part of that includes charging the right amount of dollars for whatever you're selling. The more you charge, after all, the more value you can provide, and the happier your customers will be. It's a virtuous cycle. To optimize your business for profit instead of only top-line revenue, you've got to pay attention to pricing. That's what Abby Walker, founder of Vivian Lou, discovered.

When Abby was fresh out of college, working in downtown Chicago, she fell in love with wearing high heels. She worked with women who had beautiful hair, jewelry, and clothes, and she wanted to have something that would distinguish her in a competitive work environment. One day, she came across a pair of heels that she loved and immediately started making them a part of her daily wardrobe. As simple as that sounds, she had no idea how much that choice would forever change the rest of her life.

In 2012, Abby started a blog called Mama's Shoes, which she wrote on for two years, sharing her thoughts on all kinds of footwear topics. In one post in particular, she wrote about foot sprays that were designed to alleviate pain for women who wear high heels. These products were phenomenal in concept, but at the time she worked for a company that manufactured holistic supplements and was aware of the unhealthy ingredients being used in beauty products and over-the-counter products. Some of these foot sprays had lidocaine in them, which is a numbing agent dentists use, which she thought was a great idea—except for the fact that if you wear high heels, you probably shouldn't be numbing your feet. It didn't seem like the healthiest choice in her mind, and she wondered if there was a more natural solution.

The idea never went away, and in January 2014 she decided to create her own foot spray. Abby didn't know how she would do it or what it would entail; all she had was a little bit of courage and the curiosity to hire others to help her. This team included a clinical herbalist and a naturopathic doctor who created a product that was safer and healthier than what was already out in the marketplace. Vivian Lou went into production, manufacturing the spray on a small scale, but as they tried to scale the process, they were unable to get the same formula to work at a mass-production level. Frustrated and heartbroken at her failure, Abby continued searching for better products for women with heel pain.

In April of that same year, she stumbled across a forum where two women were talking about an insole called Insolia. She'd never heard of the product, so she looked them up, found the CEO's contact information, and reached out. He offered to send her some samples of the product, and when Abby tested them, she fell in love.

She was so over the moon, in fact, that she offered her services to help him market the product more effectively to women. Her initial proposal was simple: "I'll take a cut of any increased sales." After a couple of conversations, though, Abby ended up becoming the exclusive distributor of Insolia in both the United States and Canada—a full pivot for her fledgling business, which only happened because she was willing to pick up the phone and ask, "Why have I never heard of this product?"

Abby started selling Insolia under her brand, Vivian Lou. Her husband was still working full-time, and she had no idea where any of this would go—but something was starting to happen. When she started, she was fulfilling orders all by herself, so the first thing she did after finding a product that finally worked on a mass scale was get a fulfillment center. She designed her own original packaging and website and started taking orders.

Initially, she started selling two insoles for $9.95. This was positioning the product on the same level as a Dr. Scholl's–type insert, which was not where she wanted to be. What Vivian Lou was selling went well beyond any other insole. The science behind it, the way it was designed, how it fit in the shoe—it was all next-level, and it needed to be positioned as such. The brand required visibility in an elevated space, appealing to the same professional women Abby had seen on the streets of Chicago so many years before.

It was around this time that Abby attended a business seminar talking about increasing your sales. The woman leading the seminar was Ursula Mendez, and she told Abby to double her prices, which she was, of course, hesitant to do. Any business owner who's started to see some sales come in can relate to that fear of not wanting to charge too much, but also being curious about how much you could charge. And as frugal as I may be, one place I believe you shouldn't try to "save" is what you charge your customers. Still, I know the hesitancy any entrepreneur faces when considering increasing their prices. It's almost always necessary, but doubling what you charge overnight is not something to take lightly.

Abby was scared of the customer pushback and rightly so. However, she also needed more capital to invest into expanding the business, and earning more per unit would be a quick and easy way to do that without having to borrow money. So she took a risk, biting the bullet and doubling her prices. Immediately, she received two angry emails from customers who were taken aback. And then . . . that was it. No one else said a thing, and everything else in the business continued just like clockwork. Orders kept coming in, Vivian Lou kept growing, and Abby made twice as much money as before.

Sometimes, prioritizing profit can be as simple as charging what your product or service is actually worth. But for Abby, this was just the tip of the iceberg. In April 2018, she quit her full-time job and jumped all in on the business, as it was picking up steam and showed no signs of slowing down.

Shortly after this leap of faith, she was invited to a "pitch night" in

New York City, where she met Adam Glassman, creative director at *O, The Oprah Magazine*. When she showed him her insoles, Adam said it was a great product but that the packaging didn't "scream" what it did. If she wanted the product to be in retail stores, he told her, she should rethink how the product was packaged. Inspired by Spanx, a brand that disrupted the hosiery marketplace with bold, bright, colorful packaging, Abby began redesigning the product and in August relaunched newly redesigned insoles. They were an immediate hit.

Shortly after this, *O, The Oprah Magazine* contacted her, letting Abby know that she and her company would be featured in their next issue. When she realized the story of Vivian Lou was going to be in newsstands all over the country, and the interviewer asked what the price was, she realized that she could play it conservatively or once again double down, betting on herself and finding more ways to further establish her brand as an industry leader. On the phone, at that precise moment, she made another bold decision and increased the price another $10 per unit—a 50 percent markup only a short time after having just doubled her prices. The price was $29 per pair of insoles, she told the interviewer. And it's been that way ever since.

Abby's story illustrates a powerful reality about entrepreneurship, which is that products and services have no set or inherent value. Things are worth whatever people are willing to pay. And unless that sounds Machiavellian to you, know that charging as much as you possibly can is good for you and your customers. Allow me to explain: Almost every entrepreneur I meet undervalues what they offer the world and suffers for it. The less you charge, the less you are able to do for your client or customer. It's just basic math. If you hire someone to come fix your toilet, and they charge you $50/hour but they're just barely getting by on those rates, how good of a job do you think they'll do? Will they have to rush, cut corners, overlook simple errors for the sake of expediency? Now, let's say they charge you $75, and that number represents a healthier margin and competitive rate for a plumber (I have no idea here, I'm just making this up). In this case, would you expect them to do a better job, take their time, provide a little more care to the service? I certainly would.

The same is true for you. Of course, you can't charge whatever you want; there is a point where people will just flatly tell you no. The plumber may be able to charge even $100 per hour, maybe $200. But he probably can't charge $5,000 per hour. Or maybe he can, but only for a certain kind of client. When you prioritize profit, you want to minimize expenses as much as possible while charging the right price to attract the kind of customers you want to work with who will pay you the kind of money that allows you to do a good job and stay in business for a long time.

What is that amount of money, exactly? Great question. You'll have to experiment to find out, just like Abby did. But here's a clue: The market can almost always bear more than you think it can. When it comes to Vivian Lou, I personally think they're still charging too little. Hopefully, by the time you read this, they're charging even more.

THE COUNTERINTUITIVE MATH OF DISCOUNTING

Over the course of running your business, you might be tempted to discount your products. After all, coupons and sales can cause an uptick in purchases and provide you with a temporary hit of revenue (and adrenaline). However, giving out significant-percentage discounts not only cheapens your brand (think Bed Bath & Beyond) but can hurt your profit more than you may realize. For example, a 20 percent discount can cause an 80 percent decrease in profitability!

Here's how: Let's say you sell a product for $100 with a 50 percent margin. Your product costs $5 to ship, and you typically get 100 orders per day. Doing the math, you make $45 profit per sale. If you get 100 orders per day, that's $4,500 in profit per day. Now let's say you decide to run a 20 percent sale for Black Friday. Your new profit per sale is now $25. To make the equivalent $4,500 per day, you now need to generate 180 sales. Intuitively, you think that you only need to make

20 percent more sales to cover your 20 percent coupon when in fact you need to make 80 percent more sales just to make the same amount. This is why you must be careful when offering coupons and discounts, because they can have a tremendous effect on your bottom line! Unless you can generate twice the sales you normally get, it's often not worth running a sale.

The same math applies when you raise prices. Applying the same example, let's say you decide to raise your price by 20 percent. Your new profit per sale is $65 per sale. To generate $4,500 per day, you only need to make 69 sales. By raising your prices 20 percent, you need to generate 30 percent less sales to make the same amount of money. This is why raising your prices will almost always exponentially increase your profits. We want to learn to work smarter, not harder. That's the way of the family-first entrepreneur.

KEEPING IT LEAN KEEPS YOU HAPPY

Who cares about saving pennies on the dollar? What's the point in trying to squeeze every last drop of profit out of your business? Can't you just make a lot of money and not worry too much about being frugal? I mean, sure. Of course, you can do that—until you can't. Until it becomes necessary to only spend what you absolutely must spend, because you are about to file for bankruptcy. It happens more often than people think, and typically, most entrepreneurs are unaware of what their actual expenses have to be to just get by.

I'm not opposed to you driving a company car and having nice office furniture, but these are not must-haves for a business, and they can easily get out of control. When it comes to keeping a business lean, the goal is really your own happiness. The less you have to spend, the less you have to make, and therefore, the more you can enjoy. So, a great practice is to figure out how much you need to make in the business to be happy. Remember our exercise from the previous chapter? What is your bottom-line number that you need to feel comfortable and satisfied in all the areas of your life that ultimately matter? Figure it out. You should have that number written down.

Don't do what many small business owners do, which is sell as much as they can, spend most of it, then pay themselves whatever is left over. You'll never have enough that way and always feel like you're catching up. Instead, figure out what your number is and then just pay yourself that amount in a salary. It's that simple. Then use the money leftover in your business. That way, you're never overspending, you're keeping things lean, and you're making enough to stay happy. That number, by the way, can be whatever you want—but knowing it is half the battle to feeling like you are financially in control of your business and not the other way around.

Beware the temptation to keep up with the Joneses or overinvest your capital in something that forces you to grow. One of my students, for example, decided to buy an office building, and it was larger than they needed. The mortgage on that office building was so high that the business owner felt compelled to grow the company to justify the need for the office building in the first place. Isn't that backward? It's almost like when you overextend yourself to buy a house you can't afford and have to increase your lifestyle to feel comfortable in that larger house. The same goes for business. Oftentimes, entrepreneurs find themselves chasing "success" (as defined by friends, peers, and mentors), investing a lot of time, money and energy into creating that success, then having to keep up with the standard they didn't necessarily want or need in the first place.

Another one of my colleagues invested in a large team, because she was told by another entrepreneur that this was the fastest way to grow a company and sell it, so that she could have the freedom she wanted. We've already covered the solution to this, but if you're still not convinced, make sure you look at your profit margin before hiring. Again, I want to be clear here when it comes to people: It can be really fulfilling to work with great people toward a common goal. But people are expensive and not always consistent in terms of their reliability and output. Human beings can do incredible things, of course, but investing in human capital is risky and requires a high level of commitment. Just because you are doing well this month doesn't mean you will be next month, and it's a risk to immediately staff up in times of prosperity. Make sure you've got the money to invest in such a growth strategy and some reserves to weather the storms in case of inevitable ups and downs in the business.

This colleague in particular really wanted a large team and didn't have the revenue to show for it. Still, she thought it was the only way. And in paying all these people and hiring expensive consultants, she felt completely overwhelmed. Every person she hired was a burden, another bill that kept coming in each month. Her profitable lifestyle business that allowed her to live comfortably was now demanding every dollar she made—and then some. She felt pressured to grow the company beyond where she wanted to take it just so that she could make payroll. She had set a pace for herself that was impossible to maintain and was killing her joy in the process. This is a common pitfall and in my view completely unnecessary.

If you want a business that allows you to live a good life, pay attention to profit. Keep your numbers as lean as possible, using software instead of people wherever you can. In the event that you need to scale back due to tough times, it's way easier to dump an app than it is to fire an employee. Trust me on that. Pay yourself what you need first, prioritizing your happiness above any arbitrary metrics for success. Learn to love what you have, be skeptical toward empty promises of "when you get here, you can enjoy yourself," and maximize what truly matters. In the end, all those fancy zeroes at the end of a bank account don't make you happy; you being in control of your personal life and work, however, will.

FOCUS ON CUSTOMERS WHO MATTER

Another area where you can stay lean is in what customers you decide to focus on and which ones you don't. It's not true that the customer is always right. They rarely if ever know exactly what they want, and it's your job to help make the solution to their problem as simple and easy as possible. Make no mistake: Your job is to serve them. But you are not required to serve everyone who needs your product or service. After all, every time you take someone's money, you are selling a little bit of your time and energy to them. So be careful.

Not all customers are created equal. Part of the family-first ethos is that you have to be ruthless with where you spend your time and energy, since you have limited amounts of both. Oftentimes, what you see in a business where the owners are running themselves ragged is they're not paying attention to where the majority of their money comes in. As a result, they spend too much time chasing customers who aren't worth the trouble. We learned this early on in our ecommerce business when we hit the wall. We were trying to keep everyone happy, and as a result we were making ourselves miserable.

To avoid this, we now analyze our revenue data every quarter to see where the money is coming from—and compare that to where we are spending time, money, and effort. Below is a sample of a couple of reports I regularly pull that help me decide where we are being efficient with our resources and where we are not. I'll share each of them with you, then break down what they mean and why it's important to watch your numbers. Our average order value (AOV) is about $60. AOV is the total revenue divided by total number of orders. Generally, the higher you can make this number, the more money you'll make. In a way, it's a measure of efficiency in your business, so it's a good number to watch. Knowing that, here's what we found:

Customer Distribution Based on AOV:

- 45.83% of customers spend less than $30.
- 27.87% of customers spend between $30 and $60.
- 16.30% of customers spend between $60 and $120.
- 10.01% of customers spend over $120.

Revenue Distribution Based on AOV:

- Customers who spend less than $30 make up only 12.62% of revenue.
- Customers who spend between $30 and $60 make up 17.89% of revenue.
- Customers who spend between $60 and $120 make up 20.86% of revenue.
- Customers who spend over $120 make up 48.63% of our revenue.

So, let me ask you this: Which customers *should* we be focusing on? The largest group in our customer base (45.84 percent) only earns us 12.62 percent of our revenue; meanwhile, our top 10 percent of our customers generate almost half our revenue! This is incredible news and not something I would have just known without paying attention. The data clearly tells us that we should focus more time and energy on our best customers—the whales!

We shouldn't try to keep everyone pleased at all costs. We should focus on finding more people like that top 10 percent. And who are these people? Our whales are usually event planners and wedding planners, people who need a lot of handkerchiefs and other similar products for events. These are the industry insiders who send us a ton of business just because of their size. When they place an order, it's a big one, because they're doing multiple events a year and trust us to give them a great product.

So what do we do with this information? It's one thing to know who your biggest customers are, it's another to do something about it. Every month, we go through our customer list and find people who have purchased an abnormal amount of linens, like hundreds of dollars' worth or more. Then we call them on the phone, give them a coupon code and a dedicated representative so that we can hopefully keep them as long-term customers. In other words, we appreciate them. We let them know how much we value their business and that we want to do everything we can to make it easier for them to keep buying from us.

Upon further analysis of our traffic, we also discovered that our lowest AOV customers were coming from Facebook, and the majority of whales were from a Google search. As a result, we deprioritized Facebook ads in favor of Google so that we could find more of the right people. They say the customer is always right, and that may or may not be true, but sometimes the customer isn't right for you.

Being a family-first entrepreneur is all about finding the right customers and keeping them. You don't have to work with everybody. The better you are at focusing on ideal clients and customers, the more enjoyable your life will be and the easier the money will come. Keep your business lean in terms of what you spend, whom you hire, and what customers you decide to sell to, and you will continue to have choices in the future.

CHAPTER 13

Don't Give Up Too Soon

When my daughter, Reena, was young, I decided I was going to teach her to ride a bike. Being the competitive guy that I am, I also decided on her behalf that she would do this all within a weekend, without any training wheels, and she would love me for it. Ever since becoming a dad, I had dreamed about this fairy-tale moment. In my mind, we would set a date several weeks out, circle it on the calendar, then wake early that morning ready to go.

The sun would be shining, and we'd both be cheery-eyed, excited. We would enjoy a nice, hot breakfast together, then hit the streets. Everything would be perfect. I'd help my daughter onto her brand-new, "big girl" bike that was still shiny from the store, and she'd look up at me with her loving eyes, full of admiration. I'd smile back at her, both of us knowing what a big moment this was. Then, holding her seat and handlebars, I'd give her a running start and release her with a gentle push, sending her in the right direction down the street. Grinning ear to ear, I'd watch her glide off as she effortlessly balanced herself on two wheels on the first try.

I would watch her ride down the street, squealing with excitement, as the neighbors enviously recognized me as the greatest father who ever lived. She'd circle back around as I watched and cheered her on, and we would celebrate together the conclusion of this childhood milestone achievement. Beyond grateful, my daughter would run into my arms, thanking me for yet another stellar lesson from dad, and she would cover me in hugs and kisses all the way home. It was going to be magical.

But that is not what happened. Not at all.

"Daddy," she said after more than a few failed attempts, "I don't want to learn how to ride a bike anymore. It's too hard. I can't do it, Daddy. I'm not good enough!" She cried. I wanted to cry, too. My dreams came crashing down from whatever mythical place they were inhabiting, back to earth. Back to reality. It turns out all those commercials and movie scenes where the dad is teaching his kid to ride a bike, and they're sharing a special bonding moment, are, well, *lies*. This is not how it usually happens in the real world. Where are all the scenes of the kid crying and melting down and screaming at their dad for making them try again? Where is the commercial about how the kid wants to quit and marches off, unwilling to talk to her father for the next few days? Where is all *that*?

Seeing my daughter so frustrated was hard, but what bothered me most was that she kept repeating to herself that she wasn't good enough. She wasn't good at bike riding, a thing she had never done before, and she said it so emphatically that she convinced herself she would never be any good. I felt horrible. This, I concluded, was my fault. I was the one who made her get on a bike and expected her to learn to ride in just a single afternoon. I pushed her too hard and had unrealistic expectations of the way this would go. I was wrong. At the end of this debacle, we called it quits for the day and decided to put it off for a little while before trying again.

The following weekend, I decided to try a different approach. Instead of giving my daughter a push and letting her go, I strapped on my Rollerblades and held on to her back as she rode. This way, I could support her in case she lost balance. She felt my presence behind her, which gave her peace of mind that she wasn't going to fall down or at least not fall on her own. If she went down, I'd be with her. We'd do it together.

In a way, I acted like her training wheels. Slowly but surely, I could sense her balance improving, and as that happened, she started to relax and have a little more fun. "Look, Daddy," she shouted, "I'm going so fast! Wheeeeeee!" I laughed and relaxed a little more myself while we continued to roll down the hill together. That afternoon, she enjoyed herself a lot more—doing the same thing we had done only a few days ago that had her crying and wanting to never try again. After we called it quits, she was itching to go riding again as soon as possible.

After a few more weekends, my Hollywood dream finally came true. I held on to her shoulders as she was biking, gliding beside her on my Rollerblades, and once we picked up a little speed, I let go of her back. And—lo and behold—she started riding all by herself. She was so happy at the end of the day that all she could talk about was riding her bike again. I got my fair share of hugs and kisses this time—the big moment I was looking for, even if it took a few tries to get there.

Now, why share this?

It's easy to talk about my five-year-old daughter's reaction to learning to ride a bike. She overreacted, was too easily discouraged, and quit too early. And, to be fair, I didn't do the best job setting her up for success. I made the stakes too high, put too much pressure on her to perform excellently at something she had never done before. It's no wonder she wanted to throw in the towel after the first attempt. We can all see how that happens and how irrational such behavior is. But adults often behave the same way, sometimes without even knowing it.

I bet you've done this in your own life. Be honest: How many times have you told yourself that you couldn't do something because you weren't good enough? How many times have you completely discounted or written yourself off because you didn't know how to do something? How many times have you done this without ever really trying more than once, only to realize you were so bad at it that you never wanted to try again?

This is more common than we realize. I used to discount myself all the time when it came to marketing and sales. As a Chinese American who decided to pursue engineering as a career, I was brought up to be humble, logical, passive, and never brag or embellish the facts. I told myself that this type of personality and behavior is not conducive to marketing and sales, letting myself believe I was horrible at a skill I had never really practiced.

The science of human behavior made absolutely no sense to me, and selling anything felt extremely unnatural. I hated talking about my accomplishments and having to promote my products and website. I hated the entire selling process, telling myself that I was not good enough to such a degree that eventually I believed it. After all, I had no idea what I was doing, didn't know the fundamentals, and didn't have much experience. Of course, I was bad! That wasn't the problem. The problem was that I had not given myself the chance to get good.

GOOD THINGS TAKE TIME

When I first started my blog, I expected instant results like I did with my daughter. I would try something that I learned about online, and when it didn't work out the way I had planned, I would give up. For example, when I first put up affiliate offers on my blog, I expected them to convert right away. But when I didn't refer a single sale after a few months, I immediately got discouraged and started questioning my writing skills.

When my wife and I first launched our ecommerce store, we made zero sales because no one knew we existed. No one told us that we had to go out and generate our own traffic. We weren't in a community of entrepreneurs and, like our daughter with her bike, had never done this before.

The same thing happened with my email newsletter sign-up form. When I first tried to launch my email list, no one was willing to sign up because my sales copy was atrocious. But over time, and with repeated failures, I got better at marketing myself. I improved my copywriting skills. And with each experiment, I gained a better understanding of human psychology.

What most people don't realize is that the human brain needs time for certain concepts to sink in. The instinct to pull back from anything we might fail at is a strong defense mechanism, but it ends up hurting more than helping. We have to reject the lies our own egos want to tell us—the lies that if we fail, we'll get hurt, or that if we're not "naturally" good at something, we'll never be good at it. We have to replace those lies with the truth: that we can *always* get better.

Once I started seeing a tiny bit of traction with my marketing efforts, I became hungry for more information. I devoured books, blogs, and watched videos—you name it, I did it. Slowly but surely, everything started to click. Today, I have a weird mixture of engineering and marketing blood inside of me. I honestly believe that I'm good at sales and marketing now. Not because those skills came naturally to me, but because I was resilient enough to keep learning, keep experimenting, and to build up small results over time that proved I could do them.

When starting a business, creating websites, marketing your site, or building an audience, you're going to suck at it in the beginning. The hard truth is: You're actually not good enough to succeed just yet. But you're plenty good enough to begin. The longer you keep at it, the better you'll become. In my life and in the lives of thousands of my students, I've learned that it's just a matter of getting over the initial hump of discouragement.

Once you start seeing the smallest amount of progress, you will begin enjoying the process more. Humans tend to gravitate toward activities that we are good at and therefore enjoy. Even the greatest minds started from square one and weren't that good to begin with.

BUILD UP YOUR CONFIDENCE

Overcoming doubt is a huge part of the entrepreneurial process. Like my daughter with her bike and me with sales and marketing, it's hard to try new things, and we don't like being bad at something. If you're anything like me, the first thing you do before trying something new is research. But research will only take you so far. At some point you need to just take a chance and go for it. The good news is, we know how to build confidence. In 1997, the late psychologist Albert Bandura identified four ways to build up your self-efficacy—your belief in your own ability to accomplish something.

Mastery Experiences

The first way to create more self-efficacy in a person is what Bandura calls "mastery experiences." A powerful way to build confidence is by taking small steps that build momentum and prove you can do something because you've done it before. When you start to build up a track record of small successes, you'll feel more confident about tackling the next challenge. The key is breaking your big goal down into smaller steps and finding that first small win. Remember when we talked about how to make your first $1,000? You need to do that early on and quickly so that you have the confidence to keep going, making bigger bets as you go.

Vicarious Experiences

The next best way to build confidence is by watching other people like you accomplish the same goal, what Bandura called "vicarious experiences." You can do this by reading books, following online mentors, or joining mastermind groups. Seeing someone else succeed gives you the confidence and motivation to do it yourself. Plus, you can see the blueprint of other people's achievements and learn from their failures. You don't have to reinvent the wheel.

Encouragement

The next experience on the list is encouragement. Just like my job was to be a cheerleader for my daughter as she learned to ride a bike, my job now is to be your cheerleader. I can promise you that no matter how different you might think your situation is, no matter how loud your fear might be, I've seen it before. Don't let a little failure slow you down or make you believe that you need to quit. You can do this. It may take longer than you'd like, but it's possible. I'm not selling you snake oil; this stuff works. Entrepreneurship is hard work, but it doesn't have to kill you and take time away from your family. You've got this, so long as you don't give up.

Taking Care of Yourself

The final type of experience that makes us more confident is self-care. In a way, this is what this whole book is about: doing entrepreneurship in a way that doesn't run us ragged. When you are happy and healthy, you show up as your best self. You won't be able to think creatively, make the right decisions, and give your best to your family or your business if you're burnt out and discouraged. Taking care of yourself emotionally, physically, and mentally, is foundational to your long-term success. When you push and strive, you end up robbing yourself of the stamina you need to see your vision through and truly create a business that will give you the freedom you want for years to come.

FIND A BETTER PEER GROUP

I am a self-motivated person and an independent thinker, but I've discovered over the years that my actions are directly shaped by the people I see the most. For example, when I hang out with someone who goes out all the time, I go out all the time (or at least I did, when I hung out with those kinds of people).

When I hang out with someone who is overweight and out of shape, I become overweight and out of shape. When I hang out with someone who is fiercely driven to succeed, I'm motivated to succeed. My wants, needs, and desires are heavily influenced by my peers. Before I started my two businesses, "post-college Steve" wanted to create a high-tech start-up that would go public and make millions.

Another part of me wanted to drive an Audi A4 Turbo, buy a gigantic house in Palo Alto where all of my friends could crash and throw parties, and own the latest computer equipment and gadgets as soon as they came out. Why did I want these things? Because that's what all of my friends were buying. Getting into the start-up world, at the time, was the cool thing to do. I wanted to drive an Audi A4 because it was the dream car of a girl I liked back in college. She would have been impressed. I wanted to live in Palo Alto because it's where my friends wanted to live. And I wanted to own all the latest gadgets because my friends are geeks and I wanted to impress them.

During my high school years, I hung out with geeks who cared about getting good grades, so I got good grades and got into Stanford. At Stanford, I was surrounded by other driven students, and that pushed me to pursue a career in electrical engineering. These are good things. There's nothing wrong with letting positive peer pressure put you on a better path than you would have followed otherwise. The hard part is finding the right people to push you in the direction you want to go at your specific life stage. If you're feeling stuck, chances are your current peer group is the wrong fit.

I learned this the hard way. It took me about twenty years to realize my friend group from Stanford was not the right group for me in terms of starting my own small business. In Silicon Valley, it's all about funded start-ups, and I would hear something like the following at least once a week:

"*I just raised ten million dollars at a fifty-million-dollar valuation!*"

"*I'm pulling eighty-hour weeks right now, but my company is on the cusp of a huge payout!*"

"*Steve, I can't wait to tell you about what I'm working on. It's the next big thing!*"

It's a culture of big risk, big reward. But no one ever talks about what you lose in the risk, and if it's worth giving up something you can never get back to obtain something you might never get. When I graduated college, I thought I wanted to create a venture-backed start-up because all my friends were doing the same. The desires of my peers became a model of my own. What they wanted, I wanted, without even stopping to ask if it was, indeed, what I wanted.

As humans, we tend to imitate what our peer group wants because it becomes a localized symbol of success. Is it a coincidence that five of my friends remodeled their houses during the pandemic? Is it a coincidence all my friends own a Tesla? We want what our close friends want. Or at least, we think we do. So make sure you know what you want ahead of time, before you start hanging out with people who will inevitably influence you, often unconsciously, and help define your goals and priorities. Pay attention to who you put yourself around, because whether you like it or not, you just elected the biggest influencers of your life. There's nothing wrong with following in the footsteps of your friends or even trying to keep up with the Joneses. Just make sure you actually want to be a Jones.

WHEN FRIENDS NO LONGER FIT

The hardest part of defining success and moving toward what you want is realizing when you've outgrown your current peer group and need to make new friends. Heck, it took me over a decade to realize I needed new people in my life. If you find that your friends and family aren't being supportive of your values and priorities, if they are constantly questioning your actions, it's time to make new friends.

You can't spend your time and energy constantly trying to convince those who are supposed to be supporting you of the legitimacy of your goals. At least, I don't recommend it. It's not worth the trouble. For example, if you are determined to get into better shape and lose weight, don't hang out with friends who are constantly inviting you to get bubble tea. I mean, I love boba, but that stuff is laden with sugar; it's a diabetic coma waiting to happen.

You may find, as I did, that you need new friends. And that's okay. Most people assume they are stuck with whatever peer group they have. But the truth is the people you call your friends were, at some point, just strangers doing cool stuff you were interested in. And you found a way to connect with them, becoming a part of their lives and vice versa, and now they influence many of the decisions you make on a daily basis—even if you don't realize it. You can and should be careful who you let into this position. It might mean the difference between success and failure.

A great way to meet your people is by attending live events. Over the years, I've met most of my close friends through conferences and meet-ups and other live events. There's just something special about getting together in-person, going out for a meal or a drink, and getting to experience life together. There's only so much of a person you can experience on a screen. In fact, I started my podcast for the sole purpose of meeting new people. By running an interview-based show, it forced me to chat with someone new for one hour every single week. And you know what? It worked! Many of my close friends and peers, as well as some business heroes and mentors, came into my life as a result of my reaching out to that person and asking to interview them.

We've got to know where we're headed, what is most important to us, and who can help us get there without sacrificing the essentials. It's not enough to simply have a casual connection with people you admire and respect. To really get to where you want to go in life, you've got to commit to a group of peers who will call you out on your crap and keep you accountable to your values. This means going deeper with fewer people in an intentional and consistent way.

Once you've found a group of like-minded peers, you should form a mastermind group, which is a cohort of three to six individuals who meet on a regular basis to hold each other accountable for making progress in their life and work, to bounce ideas off one another, and to motivate each other to take calculated risks. Ideally, every member of the group should share the same goals and desires you have, or at least come close, so that you can psychologically push each other forward. Over the years, I've belonged to many different groups like this, and they've all been instrumental in helping me step out of my comfort zone.

The mere presence of other entrepreneurs in your life will inspire you to take greater action. We are all influenced by our peers, and when you surround yourself with great people, you'll find yourself imitating greatness. It likely won't even be conscious; it doesn't need to be. Human beings are social animals and easily swayed by their peers, often without realizing it. You shouldn't be drifting away from your goals because of your friendships, rather, your friendships should be keeping you in line. When you keep the right people in your life and the wrong ones out, you'll find yourself breaking through artificial barriers that have been in your head. You'll do things you didn't know were possible simply because of all the positive voices in your life.

I never thought in a million years that I could create a seven-figure business without a large team. But once I saw my friends doing it, I knew it was possible with the right systems. The fastest way to grow is to meet someone who has been there before, learn what they did, and start emulating their behavior. When in doubt, surround yourself with winners, and the impossible will become likely.

How do you make a final decision on whether your friends are helping or hurting your goals? I find it's helpful to follow this simple exercise. Take a notepad or Google doc and make two lists. List #1 should contain friends/influencers who are living a life that you want to live. List #2 should contain people who are holding you back from your goals or are giving you negative energy.

You don't have to completely ditch the people on list #2, but you need to distance yourself from excessive negativity. You need to know who might be dragging you down or holding you back, so that you can set healthy boundaries and give yourself the best shot at succeeding. Meanwhile, find out where the people in list #1 hang out and meet as many like-minded people as you can in person. Form a master-mind group, meet regularly, and I guarantee it will transform your life. Surrounding yourself with the right people who are doing business the way you want to do it can be just the encouragement you need to keep going.

CHAPTER 14

Making the Most of Your Time and Freedom

People say money changes everything, but that's not exactly true. Money changes the things money *can* change. It solves the problems money can solve, while amplifying everything else it can't fix. When my wife and I started making more than we earned at our jobs, things changed for us. Not everything, but some things. The extra income didn't come without any strings attached, and I certainly had to learn to adjust, but making a larger income did allow me to feel more free.

As we began systematizing everything in our businesses, we got a lot of our time back. We no longer needed anything but ourselves to live the life we wanted. This brought a sense of security and confidence that neither of us expected. One of the weird things about financial freedom is that if you haven't experienced it before, you don't know what to do.

When I was still working as an engineer but no longer needed my job to pay the bills, I stopped caring so much. For the longest time, I wasn't getting promoted even though I did a great job. My dad raised me to work hard no matter what, teaching me that if you put the work in, your efforts will be discovered and rewarded. But that's not how it worked for me. For years as an employee, I would slave away quietly and diligently in the background, trying to not bring too much attention to myself and hoping someone would notice my effort. I wasn't getting promoted, but I also wasn't getting fired, and that was "success" to me.

Once I started working for myself, though, my perspective shifted. I started seeing things differently, stopped assuming others had the answers and trusted myself more. When my side hustle started earning me eight times the salary of my day job, I stopped caring what others thought or what they might say about me. No longer afraid of appeasing the boss or blending in, I started speaking my mind more.

One time during a meeting I told my boss flat out that his ideas were stupid. He was standing at the front of the room, presenting his ideas, and I said, "I don't like it. I don't think that's going to work." My co-worker turned and looked at me, stunned and whispered, "Dude, you just embarrassed the boss . . . and yourself." I didn't care. I wasn't trying to be mean, but I was no longer willing to be quiet. "No," I'd continued, "I don't like this idea. I think it sucks, and here are the reasons why it sucks . . ."

You know what? They started promoting me. This whole time while I was inconspicuously doing my job, trying to keep quiet, I had no idea there was another way to succeed. That attitude may have worked well for my immigrant father who grew up in another era, but it wasn't serving me. Not until I started speaking up did people begin noticing me and recognizing my contributions, and there's something to be said for that. By then, though, I didn't care.

Sometimes the less you want something, the easier it comes. Through my business, I had learned that nothing is given to you. If you work hard, keep your head down, and expect to get rewarded—people will just ignore you. You have to ask for something if you want it. Speak up if you want to be heard. Be yourself if you want to be respected.

Once I became an entrepreneur, I didn't mind attracting attention to myself. I felt free to share my thoughts without fear of being fired. Starting your own business is one of the best things you can do for your confidence, especially when you can get the business to run itself. That's the real gift of this journey: when you get to take your life back into your own hands. And that's worth way more than any promotion.

PLAN AHEAD HOW YOU'LL USE YOUR TIME

One thing I remember distinctly while growing up was that my parents worked long hours. My mom literally discovered a cure for a disease, which is her life's work. My dad had a very strong work ethic as well. It was so important to him that my brother and I avoid student debt that he actually took a second job to pay for my college education. I am forever grateful for both my parents and the sacrifices they made for me as well as the lessons they taught me about work. I truly wouldn't be here without them.

But the upshot was my parents were unable to attend a lot of my activities as a kid. I didn't see my dad as much as I would have liked. Whenever there was a game, whether it was volleyball or soccer or whatever, I would look to the sidelines to see if they were watching—and many times they were not. I remember what it felt like when I looked over, and they weren't there. My friends' parents were there, but mine were not. Why weren't my parents there? Now, that's not to say that they missed all my games, but I remember the ones they missed. I know how that felt and didn't want that to happen with my kids, if I could help it.

So now that I work for myself, I make it to all of my kids' games. It's important to me. I could certainly use that time to work more, to get ahead, start another business, make more money, do something. But that's not what my freedom is for. I don't use my hard-won freedom to give myself more work to do. I enjoy it.

Before we had our businesses and all these systems in place, I was barely seeing my wife. When we were both working full-time, I had a demanding job as an engineer in Silicon Valley, working fifty to sixty hours a week, and she worked odd hours. With Jen's job, she always had teams that were overseas, in India or Europe, and she'd have to work either late at night or super early in the morning to communicate with them. When you don't talk to your spouse as often as you would like, you start drifting. You start to miss each other, literally. You're living these two different lives in the same house and start to feel like strangers to each other.

So there was a lot riding on building our business the right way, and as you know, we had our seasons of struggle. When I was working, before we figured all this out, I would often have to skip dinner or eat on my own just because I was working so much. Once we had solid systems in place, though, I decided to use that time wisely.

Now I eat with my wife at least three times a week, just the two of us, whether it be lunch or a dinner date. We spend a lot more time together compared to how things used to be when we might go weeks without spending significant time connecting. It's been good for our marriage and good for our family. The four of us have family dinners together almost every night, we go to all our kids' events, and Jen and I spend quality time together doing things we enjoy on a regular basis. It's a good life, and I can't believe I ever lived any other way.

Before you go too far down this path of becoming a family-first entrepreneur, I invite you to consider how you'll use your freedom. Once you launch and build your business, setting it up with the right systems and processes to keep it as efficient as possible, what will you do with your time? How will you ensure that you keep your business going? What principles will guide your personal and professional life to make sure you don't get stuck simply working another job?

This chapter is all about the habits and principles that guide a family-first business and the entrepreneur behind it. Think of this as a checklist for staying on top of what you need to do to keep first things first.

ELIMINATE DISTRACTIONS

Avoid context switching at all costs. In microprocessor lingo, context switching is when your CPU switches back and forth between different tasks. For example, when you are using your smartphone to flip back and forth between apps, your processor is frantically trying to toggle between different tasks or contexts. You might not be aware of this, but there's a pretty major performance penalty every time a CPU has to do this. It has to remember where it left off with the previous task, load things back into memory for that program, and continue. Lots of CPU cycles are wasted in this process. And if it's exhausting for a machine, just imagine how much worse it is for a human.

Have you ever tried to do work on your computer only to find yourself browsing Facebook, Twitter, or Instagram, then flipping back wondering where the heck you left off? Have you ever looked at your "To Do List" and tried to tackle more than one thing simultaneously? This used to happen to me all the time. Until I understood what I was doing to my brain. Every time you change tasks, you waste valuable time and brain power.

Today, whenever I sit down at my desk, I aim to accomplish at most one or two goals for the day. I crunch through all of them with zero distractions until I'm done. And by zero distractions, I mean zero. I don't answer the phone. I don't check texts. I don't check email. Heck, I don't even eat or drink! I'm in the zone. As a result, I've been able to quickly build multiple seven-figure companies and create systems that allow those businesses to largely run without me on a daily basis. The human brain is capable of accomplishing all kinds of incredible feats, if we allow it to function properly.

When it's time to get work done, it helps to have only one thing in mind to accomplish for the day. Any more than that will cause you to waste brain power switching contexts. If you want to be productive and not merely busy, you have to find a way to block out as many distractions as possible, not least of which includes email, social media, and texting.

These little interruptions can turn a ninety-minute productivity spring into an eight-hour drudge fest where you're left feeling defeated, like you didn't get anything done all day. Freedom for me means using my time to do the things that are important to me. Blocking out everything but what is necessary allows me to feel like I protect that time and focus on what matters most.

Instead of trying to do a dozen things in a day, ask yourself what is the most important goal you want to accomplish that day. What would your life look like if you had to deprioritize everything on your list except for the most important thing? Is that even on your list, or are you filling your schedule with busy work that other people can do or that just isn't necessary right now? What this also means is that you have to fiercely prioritize. After all, when your objective is to accomplish only one thing for the day, that one thing better be important. Kill the context switching, get serious about what you actually want to do, and start creating your freedom today.

ALLOCATE TIME FOR GROWTH

Do you ever feel like you're working hard but not making forward progress? Do you ever feel like you are just treading water? I've felt this way. For me, every single week there are a lot of "maintenance" tasks that need to take place just to keep things afloat. Having a system for staying on top of all this stuff is essential.

Every week, I publish at least one blog post and one podcast episode, and on the surface, this may not seem like a lot, but it sure takes me a heck of a lot of time to figure out what to say. Every article takes hours to write, then I have to proofread and edit it as well as search for images before it can be published.

After that, I write an email blast that goes out to my list to let people know I just published something new. Likewise with the podcast, I spend time arranging interview schedules with my guests, then the audio needs to get edited along with show notes and an image, as well. It all adds up.

This is what it takes to keep the "motor" running from week to week. And if this is all I accomplish, my businesses do not grow. To grow, I need to do outreach, get featured on other podcasts and blogs, and work on my sales funnels, not to mention the time it takes to re-search and build new products. To prevent stagnation, I dedicate one day a week to the pursuit of what I call "forward progress." On this day, I do not do any maintenance tasks. Every minute of that day is devoted to growing my businesses. If you aren't growing, you're dying; it takes time and energy to stay ahead of that curve.

The other week, I implemented a brand-new abandoned shopping cart sequence for my online store. The week before that, I improved and added to my email autoresponder sequence for my course. Several weeks before that, I implemented a brand-new ad campaign. Because I dedicate one day a week to growth, I tend to finish my "maintenance tasks" much sooner, and my businesses always move forward, continuing to grow. Progress is sometimes slow, but it's consistently up and to the right. Freedom doesn't last forever, at least not without a fight.

FIND OTHER LIKE-MINDED PEOPLE

After you've run your businesses for a while, it's easy to become compla-cent and stagnant. For example, two years ago my online store barely grew in the double digits because I sat back and didn't try many new marketing strategies. It's not because I was being lazy per se, but rather that I didn't know what I didn't know. I didn't have anything new to try, because I wasn't aware of the possibilities. This happens when you stop surrounding yourself with people who challenge you. One of the ways we keep growing our businesses is by not getting lost in the echo chamber of mediocrity.

After I quit my job and went full-time as an entrepreneur, my life was pretty easy. Systems and other people were running my businesses. I was spending time with my family. And money was pouring in! It was easy and tempting to coast, so I did—for a while.

But when I began to see how everything started to slow down, I extrapolated from that how I might soon be out of a job if I didn't stay ahead of the curve. I'm not paranoid and don't mind relaxing, but a little foresight can keep an entrepreneur in business for a long time. Oftentimes, though, the experience of running a business (especially early on) can be so demanding and exhausting that you don't have any time or energy to consider new growth strategies. Trust me when I say this: You've got to make time.

One of the easiest ways to stay aware of what's happening in your industry and niche is meet regularly with your peers. Personally, I meet with several mastermind groups on a regular basis—usually weekly. By talking to other entrepreneurs, I'm pushed to try new strategies and tactics for my businesses. This isn't "Keeping up with the Joneses" as much as it's making sure the whole thing doesn't burn down without me realizing it. All businesses are inevitably headed toward failure unless the owner is constantly keeping the company afloat.

You can do this by working yourself like a dog, or you can be smart about it. Put yourself in the company of other business owners who are successful and see what they're doing. Listen to them and share your own experiences, finding ways to help each other succeed and recover more quickly from mistakes.

One time I attended a mastermind meeting where I asked for a critique of my online store. Expecting high praise about the great job I had done, I was surprised, instead, to hear each of my peers rip my website to shreds. "If I saw your website," my friend Kevin said, "I wouldn't sign up for your course." His words were harsh but helpful. The power of a group like this is that fellow entrepreneurs tell you what you need to hear and push you to get better, faster. When I got home from the meeting, I immediately redesigned my website, which led to a 46 percent lift in sales.

PICK YOUR PRIORITIES

Most of the people I know who work themselves to the bone and complain about work-life balance don't have their priorities straight. From the beginning, my primary objective for both my day job and various businesses was to free up additional time. I've had a few surprises over the years and made more than my fair share of mistakes, but I keep coming back to this north star: Freedom is the goal and time the metric.

You have a lot more time than you realize. Our goal isn't to get more time but really just reduce waste. That's what time management is, not better managing the time you do have, but getting rid of all the pointless crap that doesn't need to be done. And one of the first places to start is with choosing the right job.

I am assuming that at this point, because you're reading this book, you have a job and/or want to make more money. I think all business owners should start out as employed individuals who want more freedom. Don't burn the boats and think you will immediately start making $100,000 a month. That may not work, and it's super risky to try. Instead, give yourself a launching pad, so that you have room to make mistakes and learn.

Of course, all jobs are not created equal. For example, should you take a job that pays 50 percent more but requires you to work eighty hours a week? Or take a lesser-paying job that allows you to work forty hours? How much is your free time actually worth? Granted, not everyone has the luxury of choosing a comfortable day job, but I've found that most people tend to chase money over lifestyle, and that's a slippery slope. I've done it myself and don't recommend going down that road.

Once you start making more, you start wanting more. Every raise is soon forgotten and you start seeking even more responsibility and even higher pay! Pretty soon, you are working your butt off, so that you can stay at a job that was never meant to be permanent in the first place. Welcome to the state that many find themselves in: working jobs they hate to support a lifestyle they resent. Don't do that.

One key for me in getting over this hump was realizing that climbing the corporate ladder at my day job was not going to lead to freedom. It was, in fact, going to create the opposite—slavery. With your business, you can easily make more money working fewer hours by leveraging computers and technology to do the heavy lifting for you, and that's worth so much more than a Christmas bonus quickly spent on a boat.

Once I realized that time was the real asset, I started making deliberate decisions to focus my time on my own income-generating opportunities—and really, it started with finding any opportunity I could to get my time back. If you can, choose the job that demands less but allows you to get by while you build your dream. In five years, when your life looks completely different, you'll be glad you took the road less traveled. It really does make all the difference.

RE-EVALUATE YOUR GOALS REGULARLY

Once you have your priorities straight, it's important to revisit them from time to time. Several years back, there was a time when my wife and I got so caught up in trying to grow our businesses fast that we started neglecting other, more-important areas of our lives. We started changing up our schedules to grow our company as opposed to the other way around, and we found ourselves feeling burned out.

In fact, things got so bad at one point that we were fighting constantly and took a break from our businesses to talk about it. You know what? We realized that we were already making more than we could spend and that we needed to revisit our priorities. Believe me when I tell you that just because you get to the Promised Land doesn't mean you stay there. You've got to watch all this stuff and protect what you've created. It won't last forever; at least not without any effort it won't.

When Jen and I were forced to sit down and look at what we were doing to ourselves and each other, it was a wake-up call. We are inherently frugal people and by nature not very showy. We don't buy expensive things, nor do we need a lot of luxuries to feel comfortable. We both spend way less than we make and like it that way.

So why were we busting our butts trying to squeeze out every last dollar from the business? What was the point of sacrificing our livelihoods for growing something that was only giving us more work to do, resulting in even greater wealth that we didn't really need to support our lifestyle?

When we looked at it like that, we realized how crazy we were being and slowed things down. Every time things get out of hand now, we make a conscious effort to remember what we need out of life, what we actually want. By now we have a pretty good idea of what makes us happy, and we try to work as a team toward that, regularly checking in with each other to ensure we're still aligned.

Remember Chalene Johnson's Priority Clarity Statement? It's a long and involved checklist that helps her and her husband discern business opportunities. Should they say yes to an interview the day before Christmas? Will it take them away from their family? Is a business that requires one of them to travel three times a month worth the cost of being away from home? These are the kinds of criteria that go into making every big decision for Chalene and Bret, and those evolve with the seasons of their lives.

You created this business, so you create the rules on how you're going to run it and manage it for as long as you want.

Always remember why you got started in the first place and don't forget the purpose of your business. Circumstances can change and opportunities come and go. It's healthy to re-evaluate what you're doing, what you want to do, and why you're doing it.

Don't be afraid to change course if that's what's needed , and don't be embarrassed if you lose your way at times. It happens to most of us. Just be willing to take your business back into your hands and create the life you want. It's up to you and only you. Freedom must be managed for it to be continually enjoyed. Otherwise, it'll fade away.

BLOCK OFF TIME FOR WHAT YOU LOVE

As I mentioned before, weekends are reserved for family and friends, and there are very few exceptions to this rule. Right now, these are the only days when I get to spend large chunks of time with the kids, and I don't want to be one of those parents who rarely sees their children. Aside from hanging out as a family together, it's important for me to spend one-on-one time with my wife. In fact, this is one of the many reasons I started scaling back my time at the day job and eventually quit.

Ever since we had our first child, our whole lives have been about our kids. *Did you feed them? Did you bathe them? Did you make sure they did their homework? Did you schedule their dentist appointment? Did you remember to sign them up for piano?* For the first few years of each of our kids' lives, parenthood was all about sacrifice, and that was taking a toll on our marriage. Becoming full-time entrepreneurs allowed us to create the relationship we wanted to share with one another. But just because we were "free" from our day jobs and had plenty of money in the bank didn't mean we understood how to have a happy marriage. But I knew one thing: Time is the most valuable commodity we have, so we started spending more of it together.

In general, time is not something that automatically multiplies itself. Quite the opposite, in fact. If you don't watch it, it will evaporate. This is especially true with our most important relationships. If we don't block out regular connection points with the people we care most about, it won't happen.

Despite our busy schedule running the businesses and taking care of the kids, my wife and I decided to set aside Fridays for lunch together and left those afternoons free. It was my one free day of the week (I was still working Monday to Thursday and spending the weekends with our family), but it was worth it. This was the most important relationship in my life, and we had given so much to our kids and businesses; now it was time to invest in each other. Neither of us has ever regretted that decision and all the other time we've spent together.

What you do with those twenty-four hours is what you do with your life, and I don't know about you, but I want to spend as much of it with my friends and family as I can. Don't wait for enough time to give to your loved ones; it won't happen. Time isn't waiting to give you more of itself; it's waiting for you to use it wisely. So pay attention to the people who matter most to you. Block out special dates with the ones you love. Create special rituals and habits with your kids. Make quality time a given, not a nice thing that happens occasionally. Your life will thank you. There will always be more to do in the business, always more your customers and team members and even bosses will want from you; so make sure you block out ahead of time what you will give to your friends and family and when you will give it.

SAY NO TO THE NONESSENTIAL

I'm not good at many things, but one thing I am great at is prioritizing my day and dropping unnecessary tasks. In fact, this one aspect of my personality tends to annoy my wife to no end! Here's what our conversations are like:

> **Wife:** Can you throw away your old clothes? I swear you've had some of this stuff since college.
>
> **Me:** I've had them since high school, actually. And I'm waiting for everything to come back in style again.
>
> **Wife:** Well, the closet is overflowing right now. Please clean it up today!
>
> **Me:** What? No! Why would I do that today?
>
> **Wife:** Because this is on my task list, and I want to check it off the list.
>
> **Me:** What is the relative priority of this task compared to . . . [This is where I read off a long list of things on my plate]. Did you not want me to work on math homework with my daughter? Did you not want me to attend my son's performance? Which of these should I delete from my schedule to clean up the closet?
>
> **Wife:** AHHHHH!!!!!

Heh. Maybe we still have some work to do in our marriage. Now, I'm not saying you should say no to your spouse, because that could have negative consequences in your life (and hey, that's your grave to dig). But I do recommend putting off anything that detracts from your most important objectives (honey, if you are reading this, cleaning out the closet is very important to me . . . but just not right this moment).

Don't ever let anyone tell you to never procrastinate. Please procrastinate! Do it all the time. Put off as many meaningless activities as possible so that you can focus on what is absolutely important and essential. Be laser focused on designing the life that you want. It won't just fall in your life; you're going to have to fight to create it and defend it every single day.

As soon as you start committing yourself to random activities, it becomes a slippery slope, and you'll never get back to what truly matters. Say no as much as you possibly can to everything that is not what is most important to you. Neglect the nonessential, and if it keeps coming back to you, then maybe it needs to be done. Anyway, I guess I'll throw away those shirts now . . . as soon as I'm done writing this book.

FREEDOM BEGETS MORE FREEDOM

Achieving work-life balance is also about perception. If you can be more efficient with your time, then you will have more of it. One thing that helps your productivity is planning out and setting aside blocks of time for certain tasks. When you don't do this, your time gets wasted without you even realizing it. By providing a little structure to your activities, you may find yourself completing tasks at a much faster rate than you thought was possible, allowing you to fully relax during the unslotted blocks of time on your calendar. The more we protect our time, the more we have of it—and the freer we feel.

Enjoying your freedom, of course, doesn't mean just playing tennis all the time or sitting on a beach, chilling out. There is more to entrepreneurial liberty than mere leisure. One of the cool things about entrepreneurship is that the skills you learn in one type of business are often transferable to another. Success begets more success, and freedom can create more opportunities to succeed. As was the case of my newfound "don't give a crap" leading to my promotion at work, once I started winning in business, that success led to other businesses.

Starting in 2007, all of the businesses I've been involved with have consistently grown in the double or triple digits each year. These ventures quickly grew to six figures in their first year or two and some even started making over a million dollars a year. First, there was the ecommerce store that we launched in 2007. The following year, I began blogging about our journey at MyWifeQuitHerJob.com, sharing the lessons I'd learned about online business with others who had similar goals and aspirations. Two years later, I launched an online course, taking the lessons we learned and helping others follow in our footsteps. Then, a few years later, I launched a podcast and started hosting a live event, which continues to sell out each and every year.

Because of how we built each business, following the principles and strategies in this book, I've been able to launch each project, allowing it to scale and grow without having to give away more of my time. For years, I worked a full-time job while doing all of this. How did I find the time to launch multiple businesses? Simple: systems.

This may sound like a lot of projects to take on in addition to hanging out with my kids and wife, and initially it was. But thanks to good systems and a willingness to keep my priorities top of mind, I have tons of free time. It hasn't been an easy road, but I keep going back to the vision for why we started this journey in the first place: to have more time and freedom to enjoy what matters most.

I have to protect my time and energy and keep watch over my family and businesses if I want them to continue thriving. These habits will help you grow your own business as well. Remember to protect your freedom, so that you can continue to enjoy it.

Quitting Is Just the Beginning

After we finally got our business in line with our family life, my wife discovered her own abundance of free time and used it to volunteer at our daughter's school, where she ran the school's entrepreneurship fair. This is a program that helps kids make their own products and launch them, creating real businesses in the process.

Since we're in Silicon Valley, we get venture capitalists to come in and share lessons about entrepreneurship, and the kids get to pitch real VCs. Each investor makes small investments—usually a few hundred dollars per business at most—and the school hosts a fair where the students practice selling their goods to real customers. They get to see what it looks like to come up with an idea, present their product to investors, and sell their goods. This creates an enormous amount of confidence in the kids and rewards them for their hard work.

A few years ago, as part of this entrepreneurship program, our kids started a business called Kid in Charge. Our son was nine at the time, and our daughter was eleven. Inspired by what they saw their parents doing, they launched their own online store. Since I had already sufficiently brainwashed my children into believing owning a business was the best path to freedom (and college), they started selling T-shirts to other kids who also wanted to become entrepreneurs. They put fun sayings on these tees, like "Goal Digger," "Kid CEO," and "Building My Empire" and then started selling them as part of the business fair that year.

At first, their sales struggled. They wanted to charge only five dollars per shirt, but I talked them into charging more since I knew many people would pay fifteen dollars, easily, for a shirt. Initially, they were somewhat timid in their approach, like a lot of kids at the business fair, sitting behind their booth and waiting for customers to come by. I saw this and leaned in with a little fatherly advice: "Get off your butt, and start talking to people! Tell them the story behind your brand and how you hand-make every single shirt, throwing out any that don't meet your standards. *Sell* this stuff!"

The shirts started selling like hotcakes—at the fair and after. Soon, though, the kids ran out of prospects (there's only so many people you can ask in your life to buy a T-shirt before you run out of people). Making a few hundred bucks was fun for them, so they asked how they could keep making money after the fair was over. I shared with them my content strategies and how to attract customers to their website.

They recorded a bunch of YouTube videos, talking about what they were doing and why, sharing their behind-the-scenes on how they create each T-shirt and how they run their business. Filming a video or two per week, they ended up making over $1,000 in their first month of business. It was fun to watch them get into it and learn about entrepreneurship as they went. After some time, though, they got bored and moved on to other things. But the spark for entrepreneurship had been set. Today, our daughter is working on her second store, which is called Reena Bee, where she's selling her own jewelry online. It's going really well, and she's having a blast.

I love teaching entrepreneurship to our kids and seeing them step into their own businesses, not because I need my children to be little tycoons, but because I want them to be happy. Happiness, in my experience, comes from freedom, and the ability to choose what you want to do.

I love that my kids are getting to learn these lessons so early on. I love getting to do all these things with them. I love the work that I do now, as a coach and online seller. I love being there for my family. But mostly, I love that I get to do this, that it's even an option. I could certainly work more, find other ways to succeed, even get into venture capital if I wanted to. But monetary success, for me, was never the goal. It was always having a say over how I spent my time and making sure that I was doing the things that were most important to me.

That's my life these days. I feel tremendously grateful for it all, even the bumps in the road it took to get here, because it's all taught me what truly counts in life and what brings me the most joy. And what's funny is it wasn't the money or the businesses or even the modicum of Internet fame I've experienced that often accompanies anyone with a personal brand. This whole process of becoming an entrepreneur has pointed me right back to where I started: to family. That's what it's all about for me. That's what I do it for and what guides me and motivates me.

Not long ago, I worked a corporate job at a Fortune 500 company. I was getting paid well and was happy for the most part. But I wasn't free. More than that, I wasn't motivated. The game I was playing felt small and my potential was limited. I worked as an engineer designing microprocessors for seventeen years. My annual raise, on average, was 3 to 5 percent each year.

In fact, I can only remember two occasions when I threatened to leave for another company and I received a 10 percent raise on the spot. Besides those two incidents, however, I was stuck with modest, single-digit increases in compensation each year. This didn't excite me or challenge me. Because I didn't feel motivated, I grew bored and complacent. Unlike a lot of entrepreneurs, I didn't hate my job. I liked the people I worked with and enjoyed the work we did together, but I didn't love the life I was creating and didn't feel like it was the best that I could do.

This feeling eventually led me to place my own series of fortune side bets that inevitably led to both my wife and I quitting our jobs and becoming full-time entrepreneurs. It took time to figure out the right rhythm and boundaries for us. But today we have finally created the life of freedom we always wanted. As you know by now, I did not make this decision overnight. I'm glad we took our time getting here, because we can savor it that much more. We can really enjoy where we are, knowing what it took to get to this place. There were plenty of bumps in the road, ups and downs in the journey, and we had to learn a few lessons the hard way (or at least, I did).

Today I can say without question that I have a great life. We all do: my wife, my kids, and me. It wasn't all smooth sailing, but we wouldn't trade it for the world. Although I enjoyed my job, no amount of money could drag me back to an office building where I do not have complete control over my schedule. Having been my own employer for well over a decade, I can't imagine the typical confines of a day job. I consider a 3 to 5 percent salary increase to not only be unattractive but offensive. I remember when that felt like a really big deal, and an incredible sum of money. These days, it feels like a bad product launch.

As entrepreneurs, we don't know what we are capable of until we try. And once we know what we're worth, it's hard to go back to what we used to accept. Once we started our business, Jen and I were achieving double and triple digit growth every year, and my old raises started feeling paltry in contrast. The income from my day job became even less relevant when my blog, which shared our story and taught others the process of becoming self-employed, started taking off. It only added more income to what we were already bringing in via the online store, which was more than enough. At that point, it was obvious. It's hard to describe how life-changing this experience was. It blew my mind and made me realize it was time for me to quit, too.

In 2012, my blog-based business broke six figures for the first time.

In 2013, it made $171,000.

In 2014, it made $350,000.

In 2015, it made $712,000.

In 2016, it made over $1,000,000.

And on and on it went until I knew I had to make a shift—which was the year I made a million dollars with my blog. You see, up till this point, I had kept my career and was working double time in the two businesses we had, and I was still going to my engineering job every day. When I realized we were more than fine and that it was time to make a shift myself, I felt excited. The whole thing was exhilarating. Quitting time for me felt long overdue, but I was still torn—this was a good job that had served me well over the years. It was just time to move on. I left that job, which I remain grateful for, but never looked back. Since then, my wife and I have continued to grow both personally, financially, and just about every other way you can imagine. It hasn't all been rainbows and sunshine, but being a business owner has challenged me like nothing else in my life. And I can't believe how far we've both come in this journey.

I share this to illustrate the power of entrepreneurship. It really can change your life when you do it right. If you want to change your life, making more money can be part of the equation, but this goes beyond what you earn. This is about what you are capable of and whether you are spending your life in service of what matters most to you. If you want more out of life, including more money, consider your position. Are you currently on the path to making this happen? Is another job really the answer? To truly change your life and the lives of your loved ones, you need to build something you can call your own. You need to take full responsibility for your life. You need to become an entrepreneur.

HAVE A LONG-TERM VISION

Most people overestimate how much they can accomplish in a year but vastly underestimate what they can achieve in three years or more. With my blog, I made practically no money for three years. No one was reading my posts, and my mom routinely gave me lip service for wasting time on such a pointless endeavor, but I decided from the start that I was going to maintain my blog for at least five years no matter what the outcome. The same thing happened with Bumblebee Linens. It took a while for it to really pick up steam and become a full-time endeavor.

Even though we didn't make much money in the early days of these businesses, we had little wins here and there as we went, which was enough encouragement to keep us going. Once our businesses started catching fire, making money was relatively easy, but we never would have seen a penny had we quit within those first few months of struggle. We made good money at the beginning, but around Year 6, we hit the wall I mentioned at the beginning of the book, when everything just caught up with us, and all the success in the world wasn't worth what it was costing us. All that to say, it takes time to figure out how to build a business that works for you and your priorities.

You should pursue your business with the goal of sticking with it for at least three years no matter what. With a long-term mindset, you will be prepared to weather through any storm. *But isn't it too late to start a business? Isn't the market saturated? Don't most businesses fail?* According to a number of sources, including Duke University, the average entre-preneur is forty years old when launching his or her first business. The average age of leaders of high-growth start-ups is forty-five years old. Not everything you try is going to work out, but it's never too late to start.

It pays to experiment with different models to see what sticks and to be patient. In other words, plant a number of seeds in hopes that some-thing might grow. In the grand scheme of things, your first business will probably not be a home run, but you'll probably score at least a base hit, and the experience will be priceless. My eBay arbitrage business made $1,500 per month and was a decent "base hit," but because it wasn't scalable, I shut it down and parlayed the ecommerce skills to launch Bumblebee Linens. My blog "failed" for years until I learned how to write and market better.

As Confucius once said: "It does not matter how slowly you go as long as you do not stop." This is the mindset you must have when building a business. If you take a look at all of the most successful companies out there, you'll notice that they all share one common trait. It took them many years to get there. FedEx didn't make a single dollar for five years. Neither did Amazon or Tesla or ESPN. But they all decided to play the long game. Focus on building something of value and never stop.

I don't know what's next for you, but I hope you find a way to create a life you love, one that connects you to what matters most to you. I hope you don't settle for mere success or status or even a boatload of money. I hope you find what you're truly looking for.

Because the secret to being happy that I've found is showing gratitude for what you already have, recognizing how lucky you are to be where you are. If you're able to maintain a healthy mindset as an entrepreneur, you can run a fulfilling business that fits with your lifestyle and brings you joy. And that's just the beginning.

Acknowledgments

Creating *The Family-First Entrepreneur* was a team effort and I relied heavily on others to create this book.

To my beautiful wife, Jen, thank you for putting up with all of my crazy ideas and for being my foundation, my rock in life. You are my best friend, my biggest fan, and a fantastic editor and therapist. I could not have written this book without you.

To my kids, thank you for being the inspiration for everything that I do. When you were born, I knew immediately that I wanted to be an integral part of your lives. You make me laugh, smile, and I'm the luckiest Dad in the world.

To my mom and dad, thank you for pushing me to always be the best. I know that you have expressed some doubts over the years about selling handkerchiefs online, but I appreciate your unwavering support.

To my brother, Danny; my sister-in-law Soojung; my sister-in-law Anita Yuen; and Mark Martel: thank you for helping us in the early days of our business when we had no idea what we were doing.

To my business partner, Toni, thank you for supporting every crazy business idea that I've come up with and for being someone I can always count on for advice.

To my ecommerce mastermind group: Andrew Youderian, Lars Hundley, Dana Jaunzemis, and Brandon Eley, thank you for always giving it to me straight and providing me with sound advice. Bumblebee Linens would not be the same without you.

To my blogging mastermind group: Jeff Rose, Ryan Guina, Tom Drake, Deacon Hayes, Larry Ludwig, Robert Farrington, Phil Taylor, Bobby Hoyt, Jim Wang, Kyle Taylor, Todd Tressider, Rob Berger, Bob Lotich, David Weliver, Grant Sabatier, and Greg Go, thank you for helping me navigate Google, YouTube, and the content marketing landscape to grow my audience. My blog would not be the same without you guys.

To my good friend Mike Jackness, for being an all around great guy and for providing support for everything that I do. I appreciate you, Mike.

To MJ, for helping me produce massive amounts of content every single week.

To everyone who has supported MyWifeQuitHerJob.com and/or the The Sellers Summit over the years, thank you for being there for me. In no particular order, I'd like to thank Antonio Centeno, Ezra Firestone, Molly Pittman, Greg Mercer, Scott Voelker, Brett Curry, Bill D'Alesssandro, Drew Sanocki, Spencer Haws, Austin Brawner, Kurt Elster, Nick Shackleford, Chase Dimond, Jeff Oxford, Andrea Deckard, Erin Chase, Liz and Adam Saunders, Kevin Stecko, Tal Moore, Nick Loper, Charlie Hoehn, Mike Michalowicz, Brandon Turner, Jake Thomas, Mina Elias, Allison Lau, Dave Bryant, Natasha Takahashi, Pat Haggarty, Corbett Barr, Eric Siu, Billy Murphy, James Clear, Nathan Resnick, Neil Patel, Brad Moss, Kevin Chen, Illana Wechsler, Tina Seelig, Tom Byers, Ramit Sethi, Chad Vanags, Ed Han, Polly Liu, Vivian Chiang, Joe Hei, Matt Sanocki, Ed Ruffin, Sol Orwell, Trent Dyrsmid, Casey Gauss, Pam Cail, Alexandra Edelstein, Joe Valley, Joe McCarthy, Craig Gentry, Brandon Young, Rick Mulready, Joel Runyon, Sam Parr, Bryan Harris, Darren Rowse, Daniel DiPiazza, David Siteman Garland, Shep Hyken, Earnest Epps, Linda Bustos, Miranda Marquit, Joe Saul Sehy, Yoni Mazor, Liran Hirschkorn, Rachel Miller, Michael Stelzner, Amy Porterfield, Jasmine Star, Grant Baldwin, Reza Khadjavi, Jason Katz, Manuel Becvar, Cynthia Stine, Brian Johnson, Steve Weiss, Autumn Wyda, Ben Turcotte, Kurt Freytag, Xiaohui Wang, Jared Stark,

Nathan Hirsch, Ben Jabbawy, Ian Schoen, Omar Zenhom, Thanh Pham, Natalie Sisson, Chandler Bolt, Nathan Barry, Cathy Heller, Jeff Cohen, Chris Guthrie, Leslie Samuel, Chris Peach, John Corcoran, Jeremy Weisz, Jadah Sellner, Andrew Warner, Zach Smith, Daniel Solid, Bernie Thompson, Michael Paulson, Derek Halpern, Michael Jamin, Elizabeth Mercer, Paul Jarvis, Chuck Mullins, Robert Cialdini, Cody Iverson, Ryan Magin, Pete Sveen, Eric Cheng, Albert lee, Chris Boerner, John Rampton, Mike Barnhill, Michael Hyatt, Nathalie Lussier, Pat Haggerty, Michael Epstein, Alicia Reynoso, Pani Sabet, Ann Mcferran, and so many more amazing entrepreneurs.

To my book team, thank you for bringing *The Family-First Entrepreneur* to the world. Thank you, Roger Freet, for being my book agent and for teaching me the ins and outs of the book business. Thank you, Jeff Goins, for being an amazing editor and writer. You are great at what you do and I'm lucky to have worked with you. I want to thank the HarperBusiness team: Hollis Heimbouch for believing in a brand-new author; Kirby Sandmeyer, Rebecca Holland, and Chris Fortunato for polishing this book into a diamond.

To everyone who contributed their stories for the book, thank you for being open, honest, and vulnerable. Pat Flynn, thank you for being your authentic and supportive self (I never thought that I would be friends with a Cal guy, but you've proven me wrong). Chalene Johnson, you are an amazing person and I'm so glad that I met you randomly at an event. Sally Wilson, you are an incredible entrepreneur and parent. I hope to make it out to the UK one day and meet in person. Amanda Wittenborn, you continue to inspire me with everything that you do. Thank you for all of your support. Arree Chung, you are one of the most successful artists I know. I'm so glad Jen introduced us. Abby Walker, you are one of the most driven women that I've ever met. Thank you for supporting the book and podcast. Amanda Austin, your story was amazing and I had to share it. Eric Bandholz, thank you for being a friend and confidant for the past ten years. Jen Garza, you are easily the most humble entrepreneur I know who is absolutely killing it online. Thank you for allowing me to share your story. Joe Jitsukawa and Phillip Wang, thank you both for inspiring me to start my own YouTube channel. You both are paving the way for Asians in the media. Joel Cherrico, thank you for being one of the very first students in my course and for sending me all of your beautiful pottery. It makes me so happy to witness your success. Jordan Harbinger, thank you for helping with my podcast all these years and for feeding my escape room habit. Josh Dorkin, your story continues to inspire me every day. I hope to make it out to Maui to hang out. Neville Medhora, you are my favorite outspoken Indian guy. Thanks for years of entertainment. Noah Kagan, thanks for constantly pushing me to do better and for offering your support. Ming Wang, you are one of the most ambitious women I have ever met. Your success is inevitable for anything you pursue.

To every company who has ever sponsored MyWifeQuitHerJob.com, I want to thank you for your support. I only promote companies that I love and I sincerely appreciate all of you. In no particular order, I'd like to thank Klaviyo, Postscript, Jungle Scout, Gorgias, RPC Logistics, Emerge Counsel, BigCommerce, PPC Ninja, Seller Labs, ManyChat, Quiet Light Brokerage, Alibaba, 8Fig, Product Labs, Privy, PickFu, GetIda, Data Dive, Zipify, Helium10, Avalara, FE International, Drip, Urtasker, Shoelace, Data Dive, Airwallex, Global Sources, and 2ndOffice.

To my students and community who support me, thank you for trusting me to guide you in your business and for allowing me to share your story. I want to give a special shoutout to Natalie Mounter, Angela Right, Maria Finch, Annette Delancy, Saba Yazdani, Jason Hsieh, Yuliya Veligurskaya, Claire Carpenter, Dave Manley, Dawn La Fontaine, Kim Meckwood, Kym Campbell, Tsippi Gross, Chelsea Frank, Ron Eiger, Carmen Rivas, Jen Depaoli, and Ming Wang.

To the many friends and family members who asked about the book and offered words of encouragement, I'm deeply appreciative. Writing a book is a grueling process and every one of your comments helped. I'm sure there are people whom I've forgotten, but I've maintained an updated list over at MyWifeQuitHerJob.com/thanks.

The Quitting Quiz

Should you stay at a "good" job you find boring or go chase the latest thrill? It depends on what you want and what ultimately drives you. For many family-first entrepreneurs, the right approach is often to take your time becoming your own boss. An easy job presents a unique opportunity that allows you to make a full salary while challenging yourself at the same time.

There's nothing wrong with wanting to live the rest of your life working for someone else if that's what you want to do. But wouldn't it be better to give yourself the ultimate challenge—and see if you can start something on the side that could eventually become your full-time gig? Quitting doesn't have to be risky.

Still, there are times and certain situations when it doesn't make sense to stick with a dead-end job. When should you quit? Well, that's not so much an answer as it is a process. And this rubric applies to not only when we should leave a job but also when throwing in the towel on any project, including shutting down a business or ending a partnership.

Quitting is a process, not a destination. The following framework is one you can use to end relationships, strategies, and even businesses. Doing this right will help you gain the clarity you need to make a clear decision and hopefully put an end to some of your misery. All you have to do is honestly answer these questions, and it helps to write them down. You'll understand exactly what you must do, no matter how difficult it may be.

QUESTION #1: "AM I SETTLING?"

When it comes to quitting something, the first (and easiest) question to ask yourself is whether you are settling or compromising your potential. Are you working at a job or running a business that has a low ceiling and doesn't exercise your brain to its fullest potential? For example, let's say you are selling cheap junk with your drop-shipping business and providing almost zero value to your customer.

Even though you might be making a few bucks here and there, is selling junk with zero quality control a sustainable business that will continue to grow? Are you working a day job where you have stopped learning? Are you just going through the motions at work for the sake of a steady paycheck? Can you see yourself growing at your current position?

My friend Nathan was making a healthy six-figure income as a digital entrepreneur selling courses and ebooks when he realized that he wanted to work on something bigger. This was especially risky since he was already working for himself and earning easy income selling information products. But he knew what he wanted and what kind of risk he was willing to take, so he made the difficult decision to shut down his course business and started what became one of the best email marketing software companies in the world: ConvertKit. Sometimes it pays to quit even a good thing.

For this question, write down the following statement:

"My business or job offers the potential to grow and challenge me to the best of my abilities."

Then, give it a number from 1 to 10 where a 10 indicates that you are being challenged and growing and 1 that you are not at all feeling challenged.

_____

_____

_____

_____

Number:_____

QUESTION #2: HAVE I PUT MY BEST FOOT FORWARD?

Have you tried your best to improve your situation? Have you done everything in your power to grow your business or are you just giving up at the first sign of hardship? For most people, the answer to this question cannot be answered objectively, and you need to seek a neutral third party for a real answer.

Over the years, I've received countless emails from small business owners complaining that it's impossible to start a successful ecommerce store:

"I've tried every marketing strategy out there. This is never going to work!"

"I tried selling online, but every product I could think of had too much competition."

One time, I got an email from a reader who claimed to have "tried everything." When I took a look at her website, though, her online store looked horrible. There were spelling errors, grammatical mistakes, and the photography was terrible. It's no wonder her store was a failure. She didn't even complete the basics correctly!

When it comes to putting your best foot forward, you can't really claim to have tried "everything" until you've overcome at least a few major obstacles. You can't claim to have put your best foot forward without soliciting outside help. This principle applies to both a day job and/or your business. Have you spoken to your boss to discuss other roles that might be more fulfilling for you? Have you shared your dissatisfaction? Before writing off your current situation, make sure you've given it your all. Knowing that you've tried your best to rectify the situation is important in order to move on in good conscience. There should be no regrets.

Write down the following statement: "I have put my best foot forward to make things work and there are no additional avenues I haven't tried to improve my situation."

Then, assign a number from 1 to 10 where a 1 indicates you have tried everything in your power. (Note: The scale is backward for this question. A 10 indicates that you have tried nothing!)

_____

_____

_____

_____

_____

_____

Number:_____

QUESTION #3: IS MY WORK SPARKING MORE JOY THAN FRUSTRATION?

Are you still enjoying the journey? Are there more positives than negatives in your current work? Is your time worth the added stress? When my businesses were making four times my day-job salary, I debated whether I should quit or not. I loved my job so much that I was willing to stay despite the inconvenience of having to commute to a physical office. When my wife and I started our online store and received no sales for the first few months, the thought of shutting it down crossed my mind as well, but I was learning so much and having so much fun that I was willing to stick it out for better or for worse . . . at least for a while. It was causing more joy than frustration.

For this question, write down the following:

"My business or job provides more enjoyment than stress."

Then, give it a number from 1 to 10 where the closer you move to 10, the more joy you feel in your work.

_____

_____

_____

_____

_____

_____

Number:_____

QUESTION #4: IS THIS DETRIMENTAL TO MY HEALTH?

The word *health* for this question can apply to many aspects of your life. For example, does your business negatively impact: your own health (both mental and physical); the health of your marriage or most-significant relationship; the health of your relationship with friends; or the health of your relationship with your kids?

First, you need to figure out how each of the above situations are important to you. How much do you value these things? There's no right answer, just an honest one. Some entrepreneurs claim to put family and marriage first but then do the complete opposite. Other entrepreneurs sacrifice their own health to maintain their business and family. The key is understanding what you truly value. I can't tell you what matters to you; that's for you to decide.

Then, ask yourself how detrimental it is for you to stay in your current situation. Is your business or job worth the toll on your mental and physical health? The answer to this question requires only a number.

Write down a number from 1 to 10 where 10 indicates that your business or job does not affect your health whatsoever.

Number:_____

QUESTION #5: DOES MY WORK COMPROMISE MY BELIEFS AND VALUES?

Money often does strange things to people, and excessive greed can sometimes lead to compromise. It can be a slippery slope. As humans, we sometimes make decisions based on money without thinking about the effects on other people or the environment.

For example, let's say you started a successful business selling diamonds but later discovered that millions of innocent women and children were being exploited to mine and produce your products. Would you be fine with that? What if the company you work for is responsible for dumping toxic waste into the ocean? Sometimes our work silently kills us on the inside. Even though the money is good, you may have to ask yourself whether you are working on a project that you believe in or one that violates your personal set of ethics or standards.

Is your business or job turning you into someone you hate? That's for you to decide. My buddy Derek used to run a successful business publishing entertainment news and gossip before deciding that it didn't make him feel good inside. So he shut it down and now runs a multi-million-dollar business selling health food products. He's much happier and still making plenty of money. You don't usually have to choose between success and happiness. You can get both, but only if you start with happiness.

For this question, write down the following:

"My work adds value to the world and I believe in what I do."

Then, assign a number from 1 to 10 where 10 indicates that you feel strongly in what you do or the service you provide.

_____

_____

_____

_____

_____

_____

Number:_____

QUESTION #6: HOW OFTEN DO I THINK ABOUT QUITTING?

The answer to this question is often the best indicator of whether you should quit your job or move on from your business. How often do you think about quitting? Is it every single minute of every day? Is it only something you think about occasionally?

The most telling signal of whether you should quit is how your situation makes you feel. For example, when you think about your business or job, does it put you in a bad mood? Does thinking about your situation ruin your entire day? Does it stop you from sleeping well at night? If negative thoughts about your work consume your mind all the time, that's a leading indicator you need to get out of there.

Jot down a number from 1 to 10 where 10 indicates that you rarely think about quitting and a 1 indicates that you think about quitting all the time.

Number:_____

QUESTION #7: WHAT'S KEEPING ME HERE?

We all do things we don't want to do because we're afraid of the consequences. When it comes to a soul-sucking job, most people work because they don't know how to make money otherwise. Most people are afraid to quit their jobs because they don't have the confidence to succeed on their own. Sometimes people stay in bad situations out of obligation. I have a friend who helps run her family business even though she hates it. But she doesn't want to disappoint her parents, and she's afraid of confrontation. I have another friend who runs a business with a good friend, but her partner isn't pulling her weight. In this case, do you cut ties and risk ruining the friendship?

The best way to deal with situations involving fear of the unknown is to analyze all of the possible outcomes. If you are scared of quitting your job to start a business, ask yourself what's the worst that could happen if the business completely failed. Then, come up with a backup plan!

When my wife and I started Bumblebee Linens, our backup plan was to go back to work if our business failed. When you create a backup plan for every possible negative scenario, it makes the decision to move on infinitely easier because it takes fear out of the equation.

So before you answer the question of what's keeping you in your current situation, jot down all of the possible outcomes and come up with a plan of action. Then, assign a number from 1 to 10 where 10 indicates that there are dire consequences for quitting and 1 indicates that quitting isn't a big deal.

_____

_____

_____

_____

_____

_____

_____

_____

Number:_____

QUESTION #8: IS IT TOO LATE TO CHANGE MY ATTITUDE?

When it comes to every situation in business and life, your attitude determines everything you do. For example, when sales were nonexistent for my business in the early days, I could have reacted to my situation in two completely different ways. First, I could have said, "It's game over, man. Game *over*! No one is going to buy these stupid hankies! Screw this!!!" Or: "This sucks, but I'm gaining many new skills that will benefit other aspects of my life. Even though the money is not where I want it to be yet, I'm enjoying the journey." Do you see the difference? Oftentimes, we want to quit because our mindset is not where it should be.

If you are angry or resentful toward your job or your business, you've effectively given up already. You can no longer be objective. So before you make the decision to give up, try to list all the positives of staying in your current situation. Sometimes seeing the positives and the potential benefits written down in a document can reframe your dilemma in a completely different light.

For this question, write down the following:

> "I'm analyzing my situation with a clear and open mind. I'm not angry or resentful about my situation and believe it will be easy to overcome."

Then, assign a number from 1 to 10 where 1 indicates that you're at max anger or resentment.

_____

_____

_____

_____

_____

_____

_____

Number:_____

STAY OR GO?

If you've taken the time to think through all of the questions above and write down all your answers, then you probably already have the answer you seek. But for engineers like myself, the numbers can help us make a more objective decision. So here's what you can do: Take all the numbers you assigned for all eight questions above and tally them up. If your total is:

- Less than 20: You should get out of there now!
- Between 20 and 39: You most likely need to quit but delay judgment for a few weeks to make sure your feelings don't change.
- Between 40 and 55: Your situation is mediocre, not great and not horrible. It's a judgment call on your part. But in case you are Asian and reading this, a 55 out of 80 is still a failing grade. I'd probably still quit.
- Above 55: Your situation doesn't seem that bad. Stick it out and see if you can get your score closer to eighty.

If the numbers above still aren't providing you with the answer you need, you can assign weighting factors to make certain questions worth more than others. For example, I value the health of my family and my well-being above all else. So I always give more weight to question #4.

If your "quit score" is between 40 and 55 and you have no idea what to do, here's my general philosophy: Do you want to go through life living at 50 percent? Is 50 percent good enough for you? If you can see a legit path to raising that 50 percent to 90 percent or more in your current situation, then you should stay, suck it up, and do the work. But if your situation is already toxic, then get out of there now.

Regardless, the simple act of asking yourself these questions and writing everything down will help you achieve clarity. In most cases, tallying up the numbers won't be necessary because you'll just know based on your responses. Fear should never be a reason not to move on, because the worst thing that can happen is you spend another year getting your soul sucked out of you. The worst possible outcome is not giving yourself the chance to realize your true potential. If it doesn't work, you can always find another job. But if you never try, you'll never know.

ABOUT THE AUTHOR

STEVE CHOU is a highly recognized influencer and speaker in the world of ecommerce and has taught thousands of students to profitably sell physical products online. His blog, MyWifeQuitHerJob.com, has been featured in *Forbes*, the *New York Times*, *Entrepreneur*, and on MSNBC. He also runs the *My Wife Quit Her Job* podcast, which is among the top twenty-five marketing shows on Apple Podcasts, and a YouTube channel with hundreds of thousands of subscribers. With his wife, Steve runs BumblebeeLinens.com and hosts an annual conference called The Sellers Summit. He carries both a bachelor's and master's degree in electrical engineering from Stanford University.